The Greatest Summer EVER!!!

LOVE, Maggie

RAE MARSH

Rae Marsh

Love, Maggie:
The Greatest Summer EVER!!!!

©2023 Rae Marsh
Printed in the United States, 3rd printing
ISBN: 9798300470845

Cover Design by Gabriel H. Vaughn
Cover Art and Inside Illustrations by Neha Anwar

All rights reserved. No part of this book may be reproduced by any means, nor transmitted, nor translated into a machine language without the express written permission of the Publisher or Author.

Dedication

To my beautiful daughters Morgan and Lyla:
My inspiration. My loves. My life.

I love you,
Mom

"My mom wants us to put on a helmet for everything that I think is fun!"

Love, Maggie

May 21st

YES!!! Summer is *FINALLY* here!!!!! Oh my gosh, I cannot believe it . . . it feels like third grade went on FOREVER!!! I cannot believe how long it takes to go through a school year! My mom always says,

"Enjoy it now, Maggie, because when you get older like me and Daddy, time goes by super fast!"

She says that like every single year we finish school . . . "Enjoy it now, Maggie." OK, MOM, I get it, when I get super old like you, time goes by SUPER fast! I'm ready to soak it all in and enjoy every moment of summer break! The school year goes by sooooo slow, but summer break flies by!

Guess what? The one thing that I am SO excited about is my 9th birthday!!! YES! I turn 9 years old in 42 days! Getting closer to double-digits! I'm counting down the days that I turn 9 years old! Number nine is so fine!! Yahoo!!! I say yippee and yahoo all of the time, but ya know what? To me, they are like the best words to describe how excited I am about the summer!

Summertime is on my mind! That sounds like it would be a GREAT trumpet song . . . you know how much I LOVE to play the trumpet. "Da da da DAAA Summerrtiiiiimmee is on my miiiiiind," ha-ha. I'll make up a summer song soon, but not right now . . . I have some summer break plannin' to do!!

Love, Maggie

Since we live in one of the hottest places on Earth, also known as, FLORIDA . . . we have a pool at our house. It's not too small, and it's not too big. It's just right for our family and some friends. It's a funny shape. Not really round or square. It kinda looks like the shape of an egg! Ha-ha. It has gray and blue square things that I think are called "tiles" that go around the outside of the pool. They are really pretty. The bottom of the pool is white and we have a light built into the pool that we turn on at nighttime. The light changes color when my dad turns it on when it gets dark outside. It's SUPER cool!! Sometimes the light is green, then it changes to red, then blue. It's awesome! I'm just really glad that we have a pool because it gets super-duper hot where we live! Even though it's hot in Florida, we do have a hot tub that is attached to the pool. Sometimes we go in the hot tub when it get's cold outside. The hot tub has water that overflows into the pool. Since the hot tub has warm water, my parents have to hit a few buttons to turn it on to make the water get hot, and OH MY GOSH, my big sissy and I can't even get close to the buttons   We shouldn't even look at the buttons, actually, we shouldn't even *THINK* about the buttons. My mom and dad are always like, "Girls, DO NOT touch the buttons on the hot tub, you can blow us up." What the heck!!?? Blow us up!!!

So finally I asked, "What the heck are we going to blow up?"

"Maggie, gas is what operates the hot tub, and if you hit the wrong buttons, the gas can cause an explosion."

I was like, "WHAT are you talking about Mom?!"

My mom said, "Maggie, hot tubs and anything out by the pool need to be taken care of by an adult. You, your sister, your friends   NO ONE will ever touch the hot tub or any buttons outside, understand? No one, ok?"

"Ok, mom. I got it . . ." Geez Louise, I didn't want to even go outside after that crazy chat, let alone go swimming! Ha-ha! Since when do we have to learn a lesson on explosions the first day of summer?! But I get it, I will always remember to never touch buttons or anything outside by the hot tub or pool. Most importantly we are NOT allowed outside by the pool when my parents are not outside with us. That is a definite NO NO for ME and my friends. Always remember to never go by the pool or outside when parents are not with us kids! It's in my brain, FOREVER, I got it!! I am writing it down in my journal though, even though my mom said it 150 times this morning! Ha-ha! I know, I know, she's just keeping us safe!

Love, Maggie

I can't believe this, but I need to put *ANOTHER* journal entry in . . . it's in the middle of the day, but I have a great idea that I don't want to forget about! If my mom is so worried about the pool and the buttons, AND explosions (yikes!), why not get us a Slip 'N Slide! YES!! Let's bust out a Slip 'N Slide. Those things are awesome! You just pump air into it, have water run down it, maybe add some soap to speed things up, ha-ha, and we have ourselves a Tornado Twister Mister Slip 'N Slide in my backyard!! Yahoooo!!! I would make it look like a rollercoaster track so that everyone would be super nervous to go down the slide! I need to go on that show Shark Tank and talk to them about developing the TTM Slip 'N Slide! That's such an awesome idea, isn't it? Not sure if you remember, the Tornado Twister Mister is my favorite rollercoaster! It would be super cool to turn that awesomeness into a backyard water slide. I have such great ideas, but I will put that one on hold for now.

I don't think my mom wants to talk about us getting a Slip 'N Slide. She will say things like,

"It's too dangerous; you will need to wear a helmet." (My mom wants us to put on a helmet for everything that I think is fun!) and then tell us 100 reasons why we shouldn't get one, which is 100 reasons why she wants to spoil our fun! Ha-ha.

Love, Maggie (aka the inventor)

Rae Marsh

"Why do parents say hold your horses? I do not know of anyone who has a horse, do you?"

Love, Maggie

May 21st

It's only a few hours into summer and I'm already bored! How does that happen? Kids can't *WAIT* for summer to get here, and once it does, like 5 minutes into summer we are already bored?! Ha-ha! Well, as I was saying, instead of asking for a Slip 'N Slide, I did the next best thing and asked my mom if Cammie could come over. My sister wanted to invite one of her friends too. Her name is Annie. My mom said that our friends could come over around 1pm to swim and eat lunch. Do you remember what my favorite food is? Come on, you remember, don't you? YES, it's PIZZA!!! So, guess what my mom ordered? You guessed it . . . not ONE BUT TWO ooey, gooey cheese pizzas with extra cheese!! Oh my gosh, just thinking about it makes my mouth water! I can't wait to get my teeth into that deep dish of deliciousness. My tummy is already grumbling from the toots of excitement! Instead of calling them nervous toots, I now want to call them toots of excitement!! That's more fun, and it doesn't sound as gross . . . well, I guess with anything that has the word "toots" in it, some people may think it's gross no matter if it has the words "nervous" or "excitement" in it! They will both be stinky!!! Ha-ha.

Cammie and Annie *finally* arrived . . . Cammie had her long, brown, curly hair in pigtails like me!! Her hair looked SO cute! She had on her bright neon pink one-piece bathing suit with flamingos all over it, and the flamingos had green sunglasses on, and Cammie did too! She also had a huge straw hat on with a pink rim around the top, and she had so much sunscreen on that her face was covered in white cream. It looked like someone threw a pie in her face!

I was like, "Cammie, you look SO cute! You have a tiny bit of sunscreen on your face though. Let me help you get it off."

I didn't want to embarrass her and tell her that it looked like she ran into a white paint brush. I always try to think what I would want someone to say to me . . . Like if I had a big boogie in my nose, I would want a friend to tell me, BUT I wouldn't want them to blurt it out like, "HEY MAGGIE, YOU HAVE A HUGE BOOGIE IN YOUR NOSE. GROSS!" That would be really embarrassing.

I would want Cammie or someone just to say, "Psst, Maggie, you have a little something hanging from your nose."

My mom always says, "It's not WHAT you say to someone, it's *how* you say it." So, in this case,

I would want someone to tell me about my boogie in a soft voice, not over a loud speaker! Ha-ha let's remember to be kind to each other and try not to embarrass our friends or family. My bathing suit was a 2-piece. It was white with bright yellow sunflowers all over. It was super cute! Morgan had on a bright blue two-piece and baby blue colored sunglasses, and Annie was wearing a bright orange one piece bathing suit that had a belt around it. A belt? Yep, a belt! It was really cool as I had never seen a bathing suit like that before. We all looked like a bunch of summertime cuties ready for pool time!

Cammie got her sunscreen all soaked up into her face and body, so no more white blotches of 100 SPF, and now it's SWIM time   oh wait, is that the pizza car that just pulled up? I can spot that big red car a mile away.

"Pizza person is here mom!! Outta the pool Cammie, we can swim later, but now its PIZZA TIME!" You know I love me some PIZZA with EXTRA CHEESE!! YES! I see the delivery lady approaching the door. She looked kinda tired, her red hat was tilted, and she looked like she had delivered pizzas all day to every kid that started summer vacation. DING DONG! GG starts freaking out when the doorbell rings. We get GG situated in the other room, and here comes my mom to answer the door . . .

"Maggie, I will get the door. You know not to answer the door to strangers."

"But mom, it's the Pizza delivery lady!"

"Do you know her Maggie?"

"Welllll, I guess not mom."

"Well then she is a stranger, so do not answer the door."

"OK, MOM! Geez."

My mom is so overprotective. She always says that it's "better to be safe than sorry." I have no clue what that means, but she applies it to pretty much everything, so I get it, don't answer the door. Ever. Just let a parent or adult answer the door so that is what I will do and that's a special note to all of my friends as well . . . Always have a parent answer the door when someone is at the door.

OHHHHH the smell of pizza has penetrated my nostrils and into my brain. That's all I can think of is taking that first bite of the gooey stuff! My mom grabs red paper plates, red napkins and a few sodas for us with red cups filled with ice! Red is my mom's favorite color so everything she can get her hands on is typically red! Annie has to drink water because she has what is called diabetes. She can't have too much sugar, or she gets kinda sick to her stomach, so she drinks a lot of water. She has to check her blood levels during the day to see how much sugar is in her body. It can't be too high or too low or she will not feel well. Annie can still have candy and stuff, but in "moderation," which means she can't have too much, and she can't have it all of the time, which we should *all* do. It's really not good for anyone to eat too many sweets. We should learn something from Annie. Too much sugar just isn't good for anyone, and we should all drink water. I think I told you before that my mom drinks so much water that one day I think she may float away!! She's always telling us how good water is for us, so I'm going to try to drink more of it! Let's all try to do that! My mom actually just bought me some liquid flavor stuff that I add into my water, so it tastes like lemonade and other flavors that I actually like. I don't know how my mom just drinks water with just water in it! Ha-ha!

Cammie and I down 2 pieces of pizza, sit for a little bit to have everything settle in our bellies, and now it's time to swim!!! Yippee!! Don't worry, I didn't touch any buttons.

"MOM!!! HURRY!! You need to come out to the pool with us so we can swim!!"

"Hold your horses, I'm comin' Maggie." Why do parents say hold your horses? I do not know of anyone who has a horse, do you? If you *DO* have a horse, then we need to hang out sometime, because I have never met anyone with a horse and that would be the coolest thing ever!! If I had a horse I would name him Silver Fox, Black Diamond, or something cool like that . . . in the meantime, I will hold my horses and then we can swim!! Remember, if you do have a horse, I want to know about it!

Today is such a beautiful day! The sun is shining, the palm trees in our neighbors' yard are swaying in the wind. We have a nice breeze. It's hot out, but with the breeze, it doesn't feel like it's 100 degrees like usual! Yikkers! My mom put on some of our favorite music, and we have our white sun chairs out, and my mom buys the cutest pool towels that have blue and pink stripes, green and white and stripes, and we actually have one pink flamingo towel that we gave to Cammie for the day, since it matched her adorable swim suit!

Cammie, Morgan, Annie and I always play a game in the pool called "The Pool Game." It's so much fun! Here's how you play The Pool Game. We all stand outside of the pool deck by the deep end of the pool. Then my mom calls out a theme, like "candy bars," or something like that, and the first person who shouts out the name of a candy bar, and jumps in the pool, wins the point! Sometimes my mom will say the answer is worth one point and if it's a super hard question, it will be worth two points! We usually play to 20 points, and whoever wins the game, gets to pick what flavor ice cream we should have for dessert! It's so much fun! The best part of pool game? GG runs around the pool in circles. She won't go *IN* the pool, she just runs and runs around the outside on the pool deck . . . it's so crazy and super funny!! We have a HUGE bowl of water outside for GG all of the time! Always remember that animals need to stay hydrated too!

Ok ......Now that I explained to everyone how to play, let's play!!

"MOM! Time for the pool game ....Let's GOOOOO!!!"

"Ok girls, get situated on the deck. Lemme think of a good one   Ok, the theme is CANDY . . . Name one candy that has Carmel in it."

We all shout out "SNICKERS!!" LOL and jump in the pool, all 4 of us at the same time.

My mom was laughing, and she said, "You all tied. Everyone gets a point. Ok, line up again." Ok, here goes the next question. *My mom was thinking over what candy she could name. Thing is she LOVES chocolate, so we know she's always going to say something with chocolate in it because she always does!!* Ha-ha.

"Ok girls   Name a candy that has nougat in it." Nougat? What the heck is Nougat? I've never heard of such a thing. Sounds gross!

My sister screams, "Milky Way!" What?

"Good job Morgan, you get one point and are in the lead."

"MOM!!! No one knows what Nougat is!!"

"Your sister does! Ha-ha so she gets a point!"

"UGH! Ok mom!" I couldn't believe it! How can she give my sister a point? Nougat Schmoooogat, but I do love me a Milky Way bar . . . But what the heck, my mom needs to pick a better candy this time so I can try to win.

"Ok girls. Line up on the pool deck. Name a candy that has lemon in it."

"MOM!!! Lemon?!!" I'm wracking my brain and wracking my brain Lemon? Oh my gosh . . . I'm tooting on the pool deck!! Have you ever tooted with a wet bathing suit on? It sounds disgusting, like you are letting out a balloon!!! HA-HA!

"Oh my gosh, Maggie!! What the heck is that smell?"

"Sorry Cammie, my stomach is getting the best of me in this game. I think I ate too much pizza!" Ha-ha . . . *lemon, lemon, think Maggie*!!

Cammie shouts, "Lemon heads!!!"

"Great job Cammie, you get one point. Now it's tied up." Ok, I'm losing. I'm not happy about this. My mom continues with the game, and she continues to name candy that I have never heard of in my whole entire 8.5 years of life. About about 30 minutes, the game is over! I lose, Morgan wins!!! Yay for Morgan! That was a sarcastic "yay!" I wanted to beat my big sissy at the game! I was so bummed out as this is my favorite pool game and I lost! The only thing I can think of is to expand my candy consumption and eat more candy? Different candy? OK, that's not gonna work as no one should eat a lot of candy, bad for your health and your teeth, but I don't like this feeling! I'm so disappointed! I know it's OK to feel disappointed, but I wanted to win and I'm *SUPER* bummed out about it! I wanted to pick the flavor of ice cream after swimming. I'm really upset.

After my mom announces Morgan as the winner, she screams "Strawberry!! Strawberry ice cream for all!!" Figures, Strawberry is like my least favorite. I bet Morgan picked it on purpose because she knew I didn't like it!! UGH!

"MOM!!! I wanna rematch."

"Maggie, it's OK that your sister won the game. You don't always have to win the pool game. Someone has to lose games and be disappointed, and today it was you. Tomorrow you may win, so just keep your head up and enjoy the ice cream. In my mind, everyone wins if we all get ice cream!" Yeah yeah, whatever mom   if I win tomorrow, I'm going to pick an ice cream that Morgan doesn't like! Hee hee!

After swimming, we hung out for a little bit, and of all things played Scrabble! Remember when I told you about my parents loving Scrabble and it was an old person's game? Well now the old people game is now becoming a thing at my house! Ha-ha! My sister makes up so many words. Annie wanted to use up her only "Z" and spelled "Zombert!?"

"Annie, what the heck is a zombert?"

"It's a word, Maggie."

"I know I'm only 8 ½ years old, but that is NOT a word   Use it in a sentence is what my parents say, so use it in a sentence, Annie."

"The Zombert was not nice at the zoo today. Ha-ha . . . OK MAGGIE! IT'S NOT A WORD!"

"Exactly!! I never heard of an animal named a Zombert! Nice try Annie but that was an epic fail!"

I get it though; everyone wants to use their Zs in Scrabble, since they're worth a lot of points. Do you ever play scrabble? I am realizing that it is a pretty fun game. You learn a lot of words too. I mean, some words are made up and they don't count, but still, it's fun and it's growing on me! Don't tell my parents though, they are old and not cool, so I don't want them to think their Scrabble game is cool (even though I think it kinda is).

It was a long fun day in the sun. Pizza, ice cream, board games, and now it was time for Cammie and Annie to go home. The sun was starting to set, and it was so pretty. The sky looked like layers of different colors. An orange and yellow layer, a red and almost gold layer. It was so pretty. There were birds chirping and flying back to their nests, probably to go to sleepies. It was such a pretty night, with a slight summer breeze in the air. But it was still hot outside. In Florida it's always hot, even in the evening when the sun goes down.

After our friends were picked up by their parents, I showered, brushed my teeth, and put on a light blue pair of comfy cotton pajamas. They are *SO* comfortable! I brushed my hair, and put my hair in pigtails, and couldn't wait to go to sleep and start chasing my summer dreams. I was so tired from such a fun day in the sun! I have got to get my sleep for the rest of the summer that awaits me!! Ohhh this is going to be a fun summer break!! Nighty night friends, moon, and stars of the summer sky. Sleep tight.

Love, Maggie

"Do you ever have that happen when you have no idea what in the world happened to your hair? My pigtails have moved to one side of my head!"

Love, Maggie

Oh my gosh!! Feels like forever since I wrote in my journal! The minute I want to write something down, my eye balls start closing and I can't write about my day!! I need to keep up with my journaling though as I want to remember every part of summer break! Guess what happened to me this morning? You guessed it . . .

"GGGGGGGG!!!! NO G!! It's summer break G! Go back to sleep GG!!!" Why oh why, does my crazy dog insist on never ever ever ever ever sleeping in?! She is going to do this all summer long! UGH! I love GG, but I'm never going to be able to sleep in, then she goes into Morgan's room . . . OH wait . . . Morgan has her door closed, so G comes back and jumps all over ME again!! UGH!! G just licked my entire face and her breath smells like farts! Gross G! OK OK, I'm getting up, I'm getting up . . . I walk to the bathroom and BAM! You should see my hair!! Ha-ha!

My dad says when I wake up with crazy hair that "the hair fairy got me!" She must have spent a lot of time messing up my hair because my hair is CRAZY! It's so funny looking! My pigtails have moved to one side of my head! Ha-ha! Do you ever have that happen when you have no idea what in the world happened to your hair? I tried to brush it, but I need some detangler to spray on my hair to get all of the tangles out! I went to the bathroom, washed my hands, brushed my teeth and all of the metal on them, as I still have the lovely braces, and headed downstairs. I wonder what's in store for the day. Sure hope its weekend pancakes! Maybe we should start a thing called "summer pancakes" and make them in the shapes of the sun and palm trees? Maggie Fun Fun is the name, and don't forget I got summer game! Ha-ha!

Wait . . . is that what I think it is? The smell has already hit my nose while approaching the kitchen. The sound of pots and pans clanging as I head downstairs. Griddle on, pancakes are mixing in the bowl and here.we.go!!! YES!!! It is!! It's . . . PANCAKE DAY! Yahooooo! We are on summer break, wake up to pancakes, and if we throw in a theme park day, this would be the most incredible start to summer break yet!

Oh my gosh, I'm hoping my mom just blurts out, "Surprise! It's going to be a theme park day!!" WOW that would be amazing! I would love a quick and scary ride on the Tornado Twister Mister! Just thinking about that ride gives me the nervous toots! Ha-ha! I'm sure if I had a Tornado Twister Mister Slip 'N Slide it would sell like hot cakes! See what I did there? I threw in my favorite breakfast with my favorite ride! I cannot believe how funny I am sometimes! Ha-ha!

I approach the kitchen counter with awe and amazement at what's to come . . .

"Morning Mom!"

"Good Morning my baby, how did you sleep?"

'I slept GREEEAATT! How'd you sleep Mom?"

"Well, if you take out your Dad's snoring, I would've slept like a baby, BUT he snores, SOOOOOO I slept ok." Ha-ha!

We were laughing! My dad snores like a bear like alllll of the time! . My mom tries to wake him up to move him on his side, but then he just snores on the other side! Ha-ha!!

"So mom, What's the plan for the day?"

(I'm thinking this is gonna be good. I can feel it. It's going to be a summer day full of excitement and fun, I know it) . . .

"Well Maggie before we do anything, I need you to clean your room honey   "

Wait, wait, what did she just say? Did she just say I needed to clean my room?

"Ummmmm . . . what's that, Mom? Can you please repeat? Sounded something like, me needing to clean my room?"

"I need you to clean your room, honey. It's a mess."

"But it's summer break Mom!"

"Maggie, just because its summer break, doesn't mean we live in dirt pile." Ha-ha.

"K mom, I will clean it."

"Honey, you have to do some chores and things and help out around the house in the summer. We've talked about this before. It's your summer break from school, but we still have to make sure the house is clean. Your daddy and I work, so we need you and your sister to help out around the house and with GG. Once the work gets done, then the fun can begin, but it can't just be fun and games all of the time. OK, Maggie?"

"K, Mom."

Remember the chore 'TO DO' list that I made in 3rd grade? I only did it for like a day and that was it. I tried though; I really did. Maybe I didn't try *THAT* hard. I will do my best to help my mom around the house. Actually, I will just help her. No excuses this time! I am going to take a quick nap though. Those pancakes were filling, and then I will clean! I really will!

Love, Maggie

June 17th

Summer break seems to be flying by. I'm doing my chores like my mom asked me to do. I'm also helping my mom do stuff that she didn't ask me to do, like doing some laundry, vacuuming, changing the sheets on the bed. I really am helping! My mom started giving me an allowance. An allowance is when your parents give you money each week for doing chores. I guess it means they allow you to have money if you help out around the house. I don't exactly know what the actual definition of "allowance" is, but I'm getting $10 per week to help my mom, and that sounds good to me! I help her, and she pays me. Hmm. Kinda sounds like a job, doesn't it? What 8.5-year-old has a job? My mom will probably tell me that she had a job when she was 8 ½! Ha-ha!

Summer break has been so much fun, but today wasn't as happy as the other days have been. Some sad news to report . . . I went downstairs this morning, and I see my mom standing at the sink, staring out the window. Her long blonde hair is up in a clip and it sounds like she's sniffing, like she's crying. She's in her long white robe, drinking a cup of coffee in her "I don't do mornings" red coffee mug.

She always says "Good morning, my baby! How did you sleep?" and today she didn't say anything. Well maybe she didn't hear me or see me come downstairs?

"Good Morning Mom..."

"Good Morning Honey. How did you sleep?"

"I slept fine. Mom, what's the matter?"

"Maggie, I received some sad news this morning. I need you to sit down honey."

My brain was racing a thousand miles a second. What could be so sad that my mom didn't say good morning? I'm scared. I'm nervous. I'm confused. All emotions that it's ok to feel, but I'm feeling them all at the same time . . .

"What is it, mom?"

"Great Grandma went to Heaven this morning."

I was immediately sad and confused. Oh no, my special grandma went to heaven? We called her "special Grandma" because that's exactly what she was. She was special. She played in the pool with me, she read me books, and we watched tennis on TV. I didn't like watching tennis, I thought it was super boring, but I watched it with her because she loved it.

"What happened to special grandma, mom? I don't understand."

"Your great grandma was very old honey, and she passed away. She is in heaven now."

I started crying. My mom was crying. We held each other tight.

"MOM. I don't want special grandma to be in Heaven. I want her to be here with us."

"I do too Maggie. We were fortunate enough to have her for so long. She loved you so much Maggie, and we will remember her always. We will be OK."

I knew I needed to be there for my mom. It was so weird. I'm only 8 ½ years old, but I knew she needed me. I comforted her. She cried. This was the first time I knew real sadness. I never knew anyone that died in my family, and I knew that I didn't like the feeling, and I didn't want to feel this way, but I also knew that it was a part of life. When sadness comes into our lives and our heart, we have to deal with it. My mom, dad, and sissy talked about our Great grandma. We talked about all of the special and fun things about her and what we would miss the most. We have so many memories that we can remember. Even though I was incredibly sad and confused, I knew I needed to talk to my parents about how I was feeling. Once I did that with my family, I felt so much better. Holding in sadness made my tummy hurt. We will all go through sadness, no matter how young we are, or how old we are. We will experience many emotions in our lives, but we are never alone. Talking to my parents and sharing memories about my special grandma made me feel so much better. My tears turned into a smile, as the memories of her cute laugh, and her sipping tea, made me smile. My special grandma loved her tea. I will never forget what a special great grandmother I had. I will always remember to talk with my parents, or a close family member to help with sadness. It really does help. We can get through anything. No matter what. Healing takes time, but every day I hope to feel a little less sad about my grandma, and have the sadness just turn into happy memories of her. Always talk about feelings. You will feel better when you do. Such a sad day today, but I know tomorrow will be better.

Love, Maggie

Yesterday was the sad news day, but today things have turned a corner to happy and fun times, as I heard from Morgan that my parents were keeping a huge summer break secret! I don't know how they did it, because my dad is TERRIBLE with secrets. Literally, you can tell him something and he blurts it out like 2 seconds later! Ha-ha! For some reason, he was able to hold this one in...

"Maggie, we have something exciting to tell you . . ."

"What is it, Dad?" *In my mind, parents think everything is exciting, so I wasn't excited at this point! Ha-ha.*

"Maggie, if you could go anywhere this summer for one week, where would it be?"

"Bora Bora!? You're taking me to Bora Bora Dad?"

"Bora, Bora? What are you talking about? How do you know about Bora Bora?"

"Well Dad, Super Rich people on TV go to Bora Bora!"

"Well, we are not super rich, and we are not on TV so, NO Maggie, not Bora Bora! Good gravy

Maggie, how about this question instead . . . *If you could go to any SUMMER CAMP*, which wouldn't be in Bora Bora, which camp would it be?"

First thing I thought of was, "Do they have a Tornado Twister Mister rollercoaster camp, where you just ride the Tornado Twister Mister all day?" Ha-ha! Now, that's the camp that I would want to go to, but I know that's not a summer camp, or I would've been signed up for that one already! Ha-ha!

"Trumpet Camp, Dad. That's the camp I would want to go to. Somewhere to play my beautiful and loud trumpet allll day long, since you and mom don't want me playin' it in the house. Even though one day, I will be a famous trumpet player."

"Ummm no, sorry Maggie, not trumpet camp, though we appreciate that you are trying to become a famous trumpet player. Ok Maggie, what's your 3rd choice, as I didn't think you were going to say trumpet camp." Ha-ha . . .

"Either Surf Camp or Circus Camp Dad. I heard those are really fun around here."

"Well . . . pack your bags, Maggie! You are going to circus camp, AND, in circus camp, they have a huge wave pool to teach campers how to surf too!! There's a bunch of really fun stuff to do, not just "circus" stuff!"

"Really? Really Dad? Circus camp?! When?" Yay!!

"It starts in 2 weeks, Maggie!"

"Yippee!! Yahoo!!! This is going to be AWESOME!!!! Thank you, Mom and Dad!!!"

I immediately call Cammie to tell her my exciting circus news! I was super stoked! I asked my dad if Cammie could sign up to go to the same camp, but the camp was already full, so no other campers could attend the camp! Bummer. I was disappointed, as she's my #1 friend in the Universe, so I wanted her to be there with me. I wonder if anyone is going from our school, or who I would meet at the camp. I'm already anxious, excited and so nervous thinking about who I will meet, and if I would know anyone, and my head was spinning thinking about all of this stuff and oh no... PHWWWWWW... PPPPPP UUUUUU!! These tiny toots came out of nowhere! My gosh I hope no one comes in my bedroom, they would pass out from the fumes!

All I kept thinking about was, what if I toot at circus camp, and I know I will!! Yikers! I have two weeks to figure out what I am going to pack for camp, and if there is any way I can hold in a fart!! Ha-ha!! My dad said that we would have a schedule that includes water activities too like surfing, and waterskiing! Yay!! Can't wait! Oh boy this is going to be AWESOME!!! I wish Cammie could go too, BUT my parents said that I would meet new friends. I didn't really want to go by myself without knowing anyone, and I told my parents that I was really nervous and had that "butterflies in my belly" feeling . . . They told me that it's always exciting and a feeling of nervousness when meeting new people, and that many kids and adults, experience the same feelings. I can do this. It made me feel better that they told me that many people of all ages, can have the same feelings and get nervous. I felt weird about it, but I don't feel that way anymore. It's OK to feel weird about things that are new and that we haven't experienced. I guess maybe the "butterflies in the belly" feeling is a *good* thing.

Love, Maggie

June 30th

I wake up today and it's awesome, because . . . NO SCHOOL IS ALWAYS AWESOME!!! I love summer! The heat, the sun, the fun, the friends, it's almost circus camp time, AND . . . MY BIRTHDAY IS IN 3 DAYS!!!!! In 3 days I will officially be 9 years old. The age of a 4th grader! I can't wait to be 9. I'm getting so much older now. I feel it too. My knees hurt, my back's bothering me! Ha-ha just kidding, that's what my parents say all of the time!

My mom said that this year we would have a family gathering to celebrate my birthday. Usually, I have a party with a few friends, but she said "family only" this year. Bummer!!! I wanted my friends over, but a family party is better than no party! She asked me what I wanted for my birthday. I asked her for a bathing suit and some shorts, tops and dresses, and the 5 puppies that I ask for every year! Ha-ha.

My mom's like, "How many presents do you think I should get you for your birthday?"

And I'm like, "9 presents for my 9th birthday? Ha-ha."

My mom was like, "No, don't think so. . ."

Ok peeps, here's another one of my rules that I guarantee will catch on if I try to make it a rule. Whatever age a kid turns, that's how many presents they should get. 6-year-olds get 6 presents, 7-year-olds get 7 and so on and so forth. Wouldn't that be an awesome rule? It would never happen, but if I write it in my journal, then maybe it will happen, so I'm writing it down . . . "I, Maggie Montgomery, want to have a "present rule" in America for all kids and all parents stating that parents should buy the amounts of presents for the age of the child . . . All in favor say, "ME!"

Then all of the kids in the world scream, "ME! ME! ME! ME!" Ha-ha! I had to write that in my journal before I forgot as that's just a spectacular idea!

Love... The one, the only, the rule maker, soon to be inventor, and funniest 8 ½ year old... Maggie Montgomery.

I have got to get this show on the road with planning. I have 3 days and counting until my event of the year!!! Maggie Montgomery will turn 9-years of age! Yahooo!! I noticed today that my mom was acting differently. I was thinking what's going on with her? Like, she was taking her device into different rooms and stuff, and she never does that, so I had to investigate . . .

"Mom, is something wrong?"

"No, Maggie, what do you mean?"

"I dunno. You seem different."

"Oh no honey, I'm fine, just busy with work stuff that's all. You excited for your birthday in a few days? My little girl will be 9 years old!"

"I sure am Mom! I can't wait!"

"Are you still nervous about circus camp, or are you getting excited about it?"

"I'm excited! Still a little nervous, but now I'm more excited than nervous, so that's good."

"Yes, that is good honey! It will be fun!"

My mom kept acting different, but she said it was just because she was busy with work, so I was like ok, she's busy and I carried on with my day. Morgan and I played soccer in the backyard, and we were talking about Circus camp. Morgan said it was "lame" that I was going to a circus camp, and said that I already act like a Clown, so what would circus camp possibly teach me? She's being mean, but I *did* think that was funny! Ha-ha!

I think she's just jealous, because I will be jumping on trapezes and "flying through the air, with the greatest of ease, I am Maggie Montgomery ONNNN the flying trapeze!"

That's actually a song, but I added my name to it! Jumping around, flying around, whatever I am doing, Circus camp is going to be AAAMMMMMAAAZIIIIIINNNNGGGG!! Hopefully they have lots of pizza and disco balls if we have a party! We all know I love me a disco ball! Just because Morgan doesn't think it will be fun, doesn't mean it's not going to be fun!

My mom tells us, "If you don't have something nice to say, then don't say anything at all," but Morgan doesn't understand what that saying means, I guess!

After playing soccer, we played basketball for a few minutes, and did a little swimming. It was a busy morning. My mom made us a healthy lunch, but honestly it was so gross! Ha-ha! She eats turkey with no salt, no anything in it, it's called "all-natural turkey" and it has no taste either, so when she went into the other room, Morgan and I ran into the kitchen grabbed a bag of salty potato chips and put a bunch on the sandwich between the turkey and the bread! It made a gross sandwich turn into a deeeelicious and spectacular sandwich! Ha-ha! It needed salt and something to jazz it up . . . my 8.75-year-old taste buds need some flavor people! We had turkey sandwiches and some watermelon pieces. Oh my gosh, watermelon tastes so good on a hot summer day, and we had chocolate milk to drink with one of those super curly straws. My straw was pink! Chocolate Milk on a hot summer day doesn't sound very good to some people, but if it's really cold chocolate milk, and if you just ran or played a sport, and it's hot out, it is SO good! In my opinion, everyone should try it! It's so yummy!

By this time of the day, Morgan and I were SUPER tired! It has been such a hot day outside, and it's nice to lay down in the cool, air-conditioned house. We stink too! It's gross and my mom always tells us to shower after we swim or do sports, but I'm just so tired. The smelliness can last on my body for just a little longer, and then I will shower. The Florida heat is just bonkers in the summer. It's around 99 degrees today!

Once I get comfy on our couch, and just when my eyes were about to close, with GG cuddled up next to me, my mom says, "Hey girls, dad is working late, do you want to go to Sparkle and Shimmer Burgers and Ice Cream to have dinner . . . Just the 3 of us?"

Oh my gosh, of all of the days that my mom didn't want to eat dinner at home AND wanted burgers and ice cream instead of boring grilled chicken and plain rice? You have got to be kidding ME!

"Mom, I'm so tired, can we order food to be delivered?"

"NO Mom don't listen to Maggie, I wanna go eat at Sparkle and Shimmer!"

"Maggie?"

"Ok, fine mom."

"Ok girls, quick showers and we will head out to a quick dinner. I know you girls are tired, so we won't be out late! I'm tired too."

So we took super quick showers and got ready. I put on light blue shorts and a white T-shirt with blue clouds all over it. It's a cute T-shirt. I could do without the clouds all over it because I'm not 5 years old, but my mother *loves* the shirt, so I will wear it. I'm sure no one will see me anyway, so I'm not too worried about this baby cloud shirt. My hair was still wet. I put it up in a scrunchie, pulled it through a pink hat and was ready to go. I probably should've brushed my teeth, as I'm sure my braces had food in them, but I have no energy. I gotta go eat so that I can come home, and go to sleep, and then my birthday will be in 2 days when I wake up!!!

"Ok Mom, I'm ready!"

"Me too, Mom!"

"Ok girls, let me grab a bottle of water for the car and we can head out."

Oh my gosh, my mother and her water. She literally will not leave the house without a bottle of water. She always wants to make sure she stays hydrated, but this restaurant is only like 5 minutes from our house. My mom says we are supposed to drink 10 glasses a day!! 10 glasses? What in the world? I would float away! Ha-ha! I'm just kidding, water is good for us, and we should drink it, but whatever, I'm too tired to think about the benefits of water at the present time. I just wanna eat some burgers and ice cream! I'm STARVING!! We are finally off to the restaurant. My mom is driving. She drives like 2 miles an hour. I swear I could probably run faster than she drives, but she's always like "Safety first. That's why I drive the speed limit and that's why you girls do not have a license." Ok, driving slow is the way to go! I love to rhyme. It's so much fun!

We get to the restaurant and there is a line to get in. "Sparkle and Shimmer" is what I call it, and we usually have to make a reservation. We waited like a minute.

"Montgomery party of 3, your table is ready "

Oh, great! That was quick! The lady takes us, along with our menus, alllll the way to the back of the restaurant. I've never been back this far as we always sit in the front at the countertop area. We love to watch them make the food, but tonight, the place is packed, and apparently we need to walk 8 miles to our table! Ha-ha! We get to the back of the restaurant and make a right to some double doors . . . The lady opens double doors and it's dark . . .

Then I hear, "SURRRRRPPRISE!!!"

What?!!!! Pink, yellow, and green balloons with ribbons and a TON of confetti start to fly! The lights come on with a disco ball! My family and friends jump out from behind tables! Is this my very own surprise party??!! It is!! It is!! Yay me!!! Oh my gosh! I started to cry! I was so happy and excited and surprised! Then I realized I had a shirt on that a 5-year-old would wear, and a hat on! Oh my gosh!! This is the BEST BIRTHDAY

SURPRISE EVER!!! I see Cammie, Lola . . . Oh my gosh, Lola is here?! She moved, and she came to my party!? YAY!!! Bob, Carter, Veronica, and a few other kids from my class. My cousins, my aunts and uncles, my grandparents, my sister's BFF Annie, and a few more of my sister's friends! Oh my gosh, I felt so happy and so excited! This was all for me and what an awesome surprise!!!

"Maggie, are you surprised?"

"MOM!!! I had no idea! This is awesome, Mom! Thank you so much!"

Once I saw the disco ball, I knew it would be a fun party!! There was a huge dance floor, and about 20 round tables that were white, all around the room. The tables were all decorated with white tablecloths that had the #9 all over them. Each table had a huge #9 silver balloon in the center of the table, that was held down by one large chocolate chip cookie decoration! Each table had 8 chairs that were all different colors, and all of the chairs had a balloon on them. One yellow, one green, one pink, one blue, which matched the balloons and confetti! There were waiters walking around with mini corn dogs and small bowls filled with Nachos. The music sounded so good, I thought there was a DJ at my party, but it was a device that was playing awesome music! There was a burger station where we could make our own burgers . . . pickles, tomatoes, lettuce (none of my friends got the lettuce! I guess that is too healthy! Ha-ha!), ketchup, mustard and mayo! All the fixings for burgers, and OMG .....a French fry bar? What? We can get cheese and bacon loaded French fries? My parents thought of everything!

Then, I go to the next "food station" and what do I see? The most glorious thing I have ever seen in my nearly nine years of life on planet earth . . . an ice cream sundae station! OH MY GOSH!!! What?!!! My favorite flavors . . . chocolate, vanilla, birthday cake, mint chip, cookie dough and every topping you could think of . . . brownies, hot fudge, chocolate candies, marshmallows, rainbow sprinkles, chocolate sprinkles, whipped cream, caramel sauce and CUPCAKES too?! Holy Smokes, this is AWESOME!! AND there were Sparkle and Shimmer BUCKETS to make the sundaes in!!! BEST SURPRISE BIRTHDAY PARTY EVER!!! I have the BESTEST parents in the whole entire world!!! Yippppeee!!

We danced, we ate, we laughed, I opened presents, and we had a HUGE cake too! It was a 2-tiered chocolate cake with a ton of white buttercream frosting, and on top was a soccer player with a blonde ponytail and a #5 on the soccer shirt! It was so cool! Then, the music went down, and the lights went off.

I hear my parents saying "shushhhhhh" and here comes my mom with a birthday cake with candles . . .

"Happy Birthday to you! Happy Birthday to you! Happy Birthday dear Maggggggiiiiiiieeeeee. Happppyyyy Birthday to you! YAY!!!"

Everybody was singing super loud to me, it was so fun . . . terrible singing, ha-ha, but really fun! My mom cut the cake, and sprinkles spilled out from *INSIDE* the cake! Every color of sprinkles you could think of! Yellow, pink, blue, orange   I had no idea it was a sprinkle filled cake! It looked like a regular cake! It was deeeelicious! My mom cut the cake and I got the first piece! It was so yummy. Some of the buttercream ended up on my nose and all over my chin!! Oh my goodness, the cake was scrum-del-I-icious! I will never forget this party. Ever!

I went from being super tired when I got there, to having more energy than I ever had in my entire life!!! Oh my gosh, this is just the best feeling ever. Everyone celebrating ME! What a fun night! Whew, I was exhausted. Everyone started to leave as it was getting super late. It was so much fun to celebrate my birthday with all of my family and friends. I got some really cool gift cards to my favorite places to shop and eat. I also got some lip gloss and a few bathing suits. Cammie got me a really pretty yellow sundress with matching white and yellow sunglasses. It was super cute, and I can't wait to wear it this summer! I'm going to take some of my birthday gifts to circus camp to show them off to the campers. I hugged all of my family and friends goodbye as they left my party. Everyone had so much fun. Some of my friends still had chocolate cake on their faces! Ha-ha! The last guest left, and we headed out to the car as well.

"Thanks, Mom and Dad. That was the best party, and I was so surprised. Thank you! Thank you! Thank you!"

We got home and all I could think about was how much fun I had. I knew I would have sweet dreams!

Best.birthday.ever!

Love, Maggie

What an incredible summer it has been so far, and my party has been the best thing yet! I didn't think I liked surprises, but I guess I do! Ha-ha! Plus with surprise parties comes presents, and I sure did get a lot of those! All of my favorite things too! It's time to line up the shorts and t-shirts peeps, because your friend Maggie is loading up her suitcase for circus camp!! I don't know how in the world anything could top my 9th birthday bash! I really don't, but circus camp is only a few days away. It's a sleepover camp too! Yikes! Kinda nervous about the whole sleepover part with girls that I don't know. I'm going to talk to my parents and ask if there are other options if I don't want to *sleepover* at the sleepover camp. For now, I am ready for bed! I had a day of recovering from my birthday bash, and I am so tired from doing nothing all day! Ha-ha!

Love, Maggie

GG!!! This dog doesn't get it!! Ha-ha! Enough already G! Always jumping on me and waking me up! GG never fails to wake me up! Alarm clocks have failed me, but my personal alarm clock named GG, doesn't *ever* fail to wake me up in the morning I wake up to such a pretty day outside! I hear a loud noise outside of my window, like a banging sound. I get outta bed, open up my blinds and what is that? A woodpecker? Those things actually exist? I thought they were only in cartoons, as I have never actually seen one live in person. I scream in excitement...*and you know my mother does not like screaming...*

"MOM!!! Come quick!"

"Maggie, what is it, are you OK honey?"

"YES! You need to see this outside of my window! Hurry! Dad, Morgan, Hurry!" And you know who runs back into my room? Of course, GG is the first one there! Ha-ha! She probably thought she would get a treat with all of the excitement going on!

I hear Mom running up the stairs, and then I hear, "Maggie, be quiet! Some people are still tryin' to sleep around here!"

"Well, get up, Morgan!"

"NO!"

"Dad!!"

"Your dad is in the garage honey, he can't hear you, now what's with all of the screaming and yelling?"

"Mom . . . LOOK! Hurry, before it flies away! It's a woodpecker!"

"Maggie, honey, I don't want to burst your bubble, but that's a Cardinal."

"Mom, I know what a cardinal is. This is a woodpecker. I heard it hammering into the tree."

"Honey, your dad is hammering in the garage. That's what you must have heard. That's a beautiful cardinal though."

"O-M-G!! So I still haven't seen a woodpecker in real life yet?"

"Nope. I guess not honey, but don't give up, you may see a woodpecker one day, but today, it was just your dad hammering a table in the garage while you were looking out your window at the cardinal.. . . . Come on now, silly girl . . . Let's go have some breakfast "

I was laughing so hard. So was my mom! Morgan was in the hallway, and we told her too! What a funny way to start the morning. I'm such a goof ball! Ha-ha.

My dad finally came into the house, ran upstairs to the hallway and was like, "What's everyone yelling about?"

"Nothing, dad, apparently Maggie thought you were a woodpecker " Ha-ha.

My dad looked at us like we were all crazy and we explained what happened! He said he was all done in the garage and wanted to see if we wanted to make some French toast for breakfast, so I figured this would be the perfect time to talk about circus sleepaway camp. I'm really nervous to be away from home for 5 days. Camp starts on Monday and ends on Friday.

We get to the kitchen and grab all of the yummy stuff that we need to make for French toast. We usually have pancakes, so I don't know where this whole French toast thing came from. My dad's been watching a TV show on France so maybe that's why? Ha-ha. I dunno. We get the bread, eggs, cinnamon, and some stuff called nutmeg. My dad makes the French toast, my mom gets some scrambled eggs whipped up and man oh man, does the house smell delllicious! It smells like syrup, but we haven't gotten the syrup out of the fridge yet! Weird.

Morgan and I set the table and we each have a glass of milk. Our kitchen table is round, and we have a big window next to it that looks out into our pool and a pond. It's really pretty and GG has a big fenced in yard to run around and play in. Once we sit down at the table, we start talking about the the woodpecker situation again . . . *That was so sily.*

I asked my mom and dad if I could talk to them about circus camp, and right away, my sissy starts laughing at me.

"Ha-ha! Maggie the clown! At least you don't need to dress up. You already look like a clown! Ha-ha! Ha-ha."

"Ok, Morgan, that's enough. Maggie is going to have so much fun, now please stop teasing her."

"Fine, mom!"

Anyway, since I was rudely interrupted by Morgan, I was now able to talk to my parents about camp. I asked my parents if I could sleep at home during summer camp, and not sleep at camp. I asked if they could just drop me off each morning and pick me up in the afternoon when camp ended, but camp is one hour away from home. I told my parents that I was really worried, because I wasn't going to know anyone *at* circus camp. My mom said that each room at camp would have 4 girls total and each room would have their own bathroom, PLUS one of the circus camp counselors are adults, and they will be staying in a cabin to take care of the campers.

My mom showed me some info that she received in the mail from circus camp, which explained in detail the schedule of daily events, campers names, ages, and where they were from, and which campers were assigned to which rooms. It also listed who my roommates would be. Ok, let's look at this list and see what we find out . . . Oh wow, one of the girls is 9 years old and she's from Alaska! Alaska? Her name is Haley. Holy Smokes I have never met anyone from Alaska! That will be super cool to meet someone from Alaska! The the other two girls are flying in from California. They are twin sisters.

Their names are Emily and Emma. They are also 9 years old. There was a phone number for the campers as well. It also listed that they had never attended a sleepaway camp, and this was their first camp away from home. I got to thinkin' that if they can fly alllll the way to Florida for a camp, I guess I can drive an hour and stay for 5 days.

My mom made a deal with me. She said that if I go for the day, and still do not feel comfortable, she will pick me up in the afternoon and bring me back home, BUT she said that I will probably be having so much fun with the campers, that I won't want to come home. Hmmm, I will see about that. I took her up on her offer. If I am not comfortable, I will go home and sleep, and if I do feel comfortable, I will stay. My mom said that she will come and pick me up, no questions asked, but just to try and stay one night and see how it goes. She said to stay positive that it will be a fun experience. That's what I will do! I will stay positive and and see how it goes.

I'm so glad that I can talk to my parents about things. As kids, we really need to talk to our parents about stuff we have on our minds and why somethings may be scary to us. Once we talk to our parents, they will make us feel better. I know my parents did. Well, we will see how this whole circus camp thing goes. Until then, time to have some sweet dreams. Good night, friends.

Love, Maggie

July 3rd

I wake up this morning to horns blowin' in my room . . .

"Happy Birthday, Maggie!!!"

Yay!!!! I am 9 years old today!!! 9 years old!! I can't believe it. The day has finally arrived! My parents and Morgan brought me pancakes in bed. 3 large smiley face pancakes with a blob of butter, and lots of syrup with a big glass of orange juice and two slices of bacon! Smells so good, and my mom never lets us eat in our rooms!! This is a very special event though . . . my 9th birthday!

My parents flooded me with kisses and hugs and GG loaded me with slobbery kisses. Morgan gave me a high-five this morning, which is more than I thought she would do. She normally just grunts at me! Ha-ha! I ate up all of my pancakes with my family around me while my parents had coffee and Morgan was only in my room for about 2 minutes . . .

My mom had a really pretty pink birthday bag with pink and white tissue paper. There was a card about how proud they are of me, can't believe I'm 9 . . . blah blah blah, really didn't care, just wanted to get to the present part of the birthday breakfast in bed . . .

And I get to the bottom of the bag. It's a small box, wrapped in silver paper. I open it very slowly because I have no clue what it is. My tummy was excited, nervous, I tooted, and take all of the paper off. It's a black box. I flip the box open and it's a silver heart necklace.

My mom said, "Open up the heart . . ."

I didn't realize that it opened. It's a necklace that opens, which is called a locket. I opened up the silver heart locket, and there is a picture of my family.

My mom said, "We are in your heart and always close to you, no matter where you are, we will be with you." My mom starts crying! Oh my gosh mom, are those happy tears? YIKES how do I react to this one? It's a birthday, we are supposed to be happy!

"Mom, you ok?"

"I just can't believe you are 9 years old already Maggie. These are happy tears . . ."

Then my dad busts out another box and says, "This is for you too, Maggie!"

I open this one super-fast because if my dad handed it to me, I know he's not going to give me a crying present ha-ha! I open it . . . two tickets to the Championship Soccer game?!! YAY!!!! This is awesome!!!!

"Thank you so much Dad!"

I knew my dad would come through with a cool gift!! I'm so happy! I love soccer with my Dad! This is going to be great!

Morgan's like, "Where's my ticket?" OOPS! Ha-ha! Sometimes you just gotta have one-on-one time with a parent, and it's OK to spend time alone with them! I was excited for it to be just me and Dad!

I was thinking   I guess I'm not getting those 5 puppies that I wanted   maybe next year? A girl can dream! Ha-ha!

After my birthday breakfast, we all hung out around the house and went swimming in our pool. It was so much fun!! Just the 4 of us! We are always with our friends, so it was really nice to just hang out with my parents and sister today, and GG! We ate cheese doodles, chips and dips, and grilled out cheeseburgers and my mom made tater tots in the oven   It was so good. My birthday cookout was awesome!

After we cooked out, my mom brought out a large cake with white buttercream icing in the shape of a HUGE soccer ball! It said "Happy 9th Birthday Maggie" in red letters and there was ONE number 9 candle for me to blow out. My family sang the "Happy Birthday" song. I wish I had my trumpet to play the song while they sang! Ha-ha.

The icing around the bottom of the cake was green just like the grass on the soccer field. After we ate the green frosting, our tongues and lips were green too!! We also had chocolate and vanilla ice cream and one of my very favorites . . . mint chocolate chip! Yummy! It was such a perfect birthday! The weather was so nice, and the pool was so warm! It was just awesome! I'm so thankful to have such a caring family. I can't believe I'm 9 years old! I do feel older because I did get tired earlier than usual, and my parents always say when they get older, they get tired! Ha-ha. This is finally what 9 feels like and I love it!

Goodnight, sleep tight and don't let the bed bugs bite!

Love, Maggie

July 15th

I'm so excited to leave for summer camp today!!! I have clothes allllll over my bed and, all over my closet. Eeks! I'm trying to figure out what to pack for circus camp. YES, in case you were wondering, I already packed my clown costume! Ha-Ha! Just kidding! My mom was in my room trying to help me pack as we are leaving in 3 short hours.

"Maggie. I told you not to procrastinate. I wanted all of your things to have been packed and ready to go yesterday." My mom was not happy with me. She likes to get things done and not put things off. My mom uses the word "procrastinate" a lot. It means to delay doing things that we should get done right away. My dad likes to put things off, so I tend to like him more during vacation planning!

"I know Mom, I'm sorry I just couldn't decide what to bring . . ."

"Hurry Maggie, we need to leave in less than 3 hours. Please go down the list and make sure you have everything. Pack deodorant too so you aren't stinky!"

We were laughing. My mom was panicking about my packing, but still made me laugh. 9-year-olds should pack double deodorant. ESPECIALLY the stinky boys!! UGH! Boys are so gross and smelly! Ha-ha! Ok, double deodorant just to be safe from stinkiness! No one wants to be a stinky head!

I'm all packed and ready to go!! Let's do this!! Let's get on trapezes and trampolines and elephants . . . wait! Are there elephants at the circus camp? There are elephants at the circus?! YIKES! I guess we will soon find out! I'm not even going to ask my mother about elephant rides! If I even put that thought in her head, she will turn the car around to get my helmet from home or buy me a helmet on the way to camp!!! Ha-ha!

After about 70 minutes in the car, we arrive at circus camp. We could see a huge pink, red and blue circus tent when we arrived with gold letters that said, "Welcome to Circus camp boys and girls."

It's CIRCUS SUMMER CAMP GO TIME!!! Watch out clowns and people dressed like clowns, because Maggie fun fun, will be flyin' through the air soon! Yippee!!!

We arrived at camp close to dinner time and drove down a long dirt road. The circus tent seemed like it was close, but we had to drive about 2 minutes to get to the tent. There was a tall guy at the security gate. He had a name tag on, and his name was Jack.

"Howdy campers! I need to see your license and camp registration please." He was checking to make sure we were registered for camp. "Welcome, Montgomery family. You are all set. Here is your key. Please follow the signs to Cabin D and enjoy Circus Camp!"

Once he checked us in, and handed us our key for Cabin D, he hit a button to open up the red and white striped gate which led to another road to the camp. The road was super bumpy and bringing up dust on all 4 sides of the car.

My mom's like, "I shouldn't have gotten my car washed today!" And I was in the backseat laughing and my rear-end was flying all over the place. I had my seat belt on of course, but the road was so bumpy, I couldn't stay in my seat! I couldn't see anything around me but dirt dust! After about 30 seconds of bumps, I had to pee!! Ha-ha!

The road got smoother when the dirt road changed to cement or whatever kind of road it is that we normally drive on. There was a sign with a bunch of different colors and arrows pointing different directions. The top said "Camper Cabins," then the first arrow was blue and pointed to the right and said, "Camper Group A," the second arrow was yellow and pointed to the left and said "Camper Group B. . ." I was "Camper Group D," so we look down the list of arrows and there it is. The bright PINK arrow pointing to the left! Yay! My favorite color is PINK!

One step closer to getting to our cabin. We see one cabin to the left that said, "Group B," Then the next Cabin that said "Group D." Yay! That's me!

My mom parks the car, and we get out and stretch our legs and arms. We needed a good stretch after being in the car for over an hour. AHHHHH quick stretch with the arms . . . quick stretch of the legs and back, and I'm brand new!

We got my bags out of the car. I only had one purple duffle bag and one small purple and white polka dotted suitcase. We had so much water in the car too since my mom is a crazy water lady, so I had to run to the bathroom!!!

The cabin was really cute. It was a log cabin. Looking at it, there was a large window in the front, and then next to the window there were 3 stairs that led up to a door. To the right of the door there was a white board that said: "Welcome Circus Campers: Maggie, Emma, Emily and Haley." There was also a pot of flowers next to the door in a flowerpot. I went to smell them and BAM, water shot out of the flowers!! What?!! Ha-ha! I guess that's the start of circus camp!! That was too funny! My face was soaked! Ha-ha! Good One Circus Camp, You got me! Circus camp one, Maggie zero!

We got all of my stuff outta the car, and headed into the cabin. It was so cute! There was a round white table with a painting of a circus tent in the center of the table. Such pretty colors of pink, blue, white and red. It was really cool. There were 6 chairs around the table which were all different colors, and they were in the shape of popcorn buckets! The seats were red, the back was a solid white and red stripe and the top was a big ball shaped like a huge piece of popcorn!! It was so awesome!! There was a button on the chair and if you pressed it, a buttery smell came out! Super cool!! We also had our own refrigerator which was a bright sky-blue color and my mom filled two shelves with water. In the area next to the kitchen there were 2 red couches, and each one had a small white table next to them with a medium size lamp shaped like an elephant. The light bulb was sitting on the elephants trunk!! Ha-ha! It was SO CUTE! This place was so crazy!! It was awesome!!

But . . . wait . . . what was I missing here? Where's the TV? Ummmm . . .

"Mother, where is the TV?"

"Oh Maggie, didn't I tell you? No TV at camp this week."

Wait, what did she say? I am feeling dizzy. I think I need to sit down. Did my mom just say that we don't have a TV for 5 days?!!

"Mom! What do you mean, no TV?"

"Maggie, at camp they want you to focus on meeting new friends, having new experiences, and TALKING to people. Kids spend so much time watching TV and being on devices that no one converses anymore. This will be great for you! You love to talk!"

"Mom, what the heck does converse mean?"

"It means to have a conversation, Maggie! Do your favorite thing . . . to talk!" Ha-ha.

Yeah, I love to talk, but not to strangers for 5 days at camp.

"Mom, does that offer still stand about me coming home if I don't feel comfortable?"

"Yes, it does, but it doesn't apply to the fact that there is no TV. You can't come home to watch TV. Understand?"

"Yes, Mother, I understand."

After my brain was trying to process the fact that there was NO TV in this place, I wanted to see the bedrooms. Just a few steps away from the couches, there was one room on the left with 2 bunk beds! Yay! I LOVE bunk beds!! The other bedroom had a note on the door that said, "Miss Meatball's room." You have GOT to be kidding me . . . There is no way that there is someone named Miss Meatball in this world!! Now I want to change my name to "Ranch Dressing Maggie" and hang that on the door. If I could change my name, it would either be to "Maggie Fun Fun" OR "Ranch Dressing Maggie!" Ha-ha!

I picked one of the top bunks. The room was adorable. It had pink walls with white bunk beds and the bedding was light blue. There were hanging lights that were lit on the ceiling and they were white LED lights. It reminded me of something you would see or read about in a circus tent. The camp really had the circus camp theme nailed down! So far, it's awesome! I walked up a ladder and onto my bunk and it was soooo comfortable. The pillow was nice and comfy, and the comforter had a tag that said, "All has been sanitized and cleaned for your comfort" and boy, was it nice and fresh smelling like fresh air! The pillows looked like cotton candy! The bathroom connected to our room. It was kinda small, but

we didn't need anything too big. The cabin smelled really good too. Nice and fresh like roses.

I was there for about 5 minutes and my mom was helping me unpack. All of us had our own dressers to put our clothes in. Just when we were nearly done unpacking, I hear someone open the door . . .

"Hello? Anyone in here?"

"I'm in here!"

"Whose I'm?" Ha-ha!

"Maggie. Maggie Montgomery."

"HI Maggie!! I'm Emily, and this is my sister, Emma. Nice to meet you!"

They are twins and literally look exactly alike! They are about the same height as me, height of short! Ha-ha! They both have long, light brown hair down to their shoulders, with a reddish tint from the sun, and bright blue eyes. Emma wears glasses that have a blue rim around them, that's like the only way I can tell them apart. Thank goodness Emma wears glasses! Emma had on a red romper with white stars all over it and Emily had a romper on too, but hers was black and had yellow bananas all over it! I thought the bananas were so cute! The girls seemed super nice and friendly. Emma and Emily's Mom flew out to camp with them from California. They also brought their little bother, Jackson. They call him Jax. He's 5 years old. He wanted to stay at circus camp, but all campers had to be at least 9-years old. The camp was only for 9 and 10-year-old girls and boys.

   After my mom and I unpacked and got things situated, Emma and Emily also unpacked in the room and got all of their stuff organized. Emily had to bring an inhaler because she has asthma. Sometimes if kids have difficulty breathing from sports or allergies or anything really, they need an inhaler, so it's easier for them to breathe. I know this, because I asked my mom about it a couple of years ago. My mom has an inhaler and carries it when she runs, and she also has one in her purse because she has asthma, too. I don't know why some kids don't want people to see their inhaler? It's nothing to be embarrassed about- it helps to breath! It's a good thing!

   After a few minutes, there was a knock at the door, and Haley has arrived. She said it took her 24 hours to get to Circus camp because her flights from Alaska were all delayed and she had to take 5 planes to get to Florida!! Holy Macaroni!! Haley said she was tired. She had curly red hair that was up in a high ponytail, and had on yellow and white striped shorts, a white t-shirt and an oversized dark blue sweatshirt with a polar bear on it! I love polar bears! They must sell a lot of those sweatshirts in Alaska. Her mom and dad brought her and planned to stay down the street at a hotel for the week until circus camp was over. It's too far for them to fly home and back again.

Haley took the bottom bunk under me. The first thing she said was, "Maggie, you better not fart up there!" It's like she already knew me! Ha-ha!

"Oh my gosh, I won't. That's disgusting!" Little did she know I toot constantly! She will find out soon enough though!

As we were laughing and carrying on in our room, our parents were in the room without the TV, talking a bit and getting to know each other a little better, and we went into the kitchen to put the snacks away into the kitchen cabinets. The cabins do not have stoves or ovens. That would be dangerous. Never EVER cook without parents being home. Never turn on the oven or stove. Ever. We only have refrigerators with a freezer, cabinets for snacks, and a sink and soap for hand washing. Our parents stocked us up with paper plates, paper cups and all that kinda stuff. We had a ton of snacks like cheese doodles, apples, grapes, carrots and some chocolate candies! Yummmyyyy!! The candies have "M"s on them so that must mean they are "Maggies!" Ha-ha!

We hear a trumpet playing over a loudspeaker "Da Da Da Da . . ." as all campers have a speaker in each cabin.

"All campers, please report to the circus kitchen tent in 5 minutes."

The kitchen tent is behind our cabin. There was a large color-coded map on our kitchen table that showed all of the places at the camp.

The four of us headed out the door with our parents and walked about 50 Yards to the circus kitchen, not far at all. We pass a few cabins on the way to the tent, and all cabins look the same. The pathway kinda smelled a little like poop, BUT . . . I'm thinking it's because of the circus animals. Let's hope it's the animals and not the campers! Ha-ha!

The tent was big and white, with flags sticking up all around it. The flags had all different colors and went alllll the way around the tent and was the shape of a circle. Seems like everything here is the shape of a circle. There were two large glass doors that opened into the tent. When we walked in, there were round tables and each table had a letter in the middle . . .

"All campers, if you would please find your cabin letter located on a table and have a seat." Once we located "Cabin D," we all sat together.

"Welcome, all campers, to Skippidity Dippidity Dooooo Circus Camp!"

Oh my gosh, I had NO clue what this camp was called! My mom just called it circus camp. First Miss Meatball and now Skippidity Dippity Doooo? I love this place! So far, it's hilarious!!

"Campers, my name is Miss Meatball, I am from Georgia, and we are so excited to have you at circus camp for the next 5 days. Each of your cabins have a designated circus camp counselor. These counselors will stay with you in your cabins. The counselors are adults and are certified in all camp activities. Does anyone have any questions so far?"

I was just thinking that Miss Meatball was really loud and didn't take a breath during her speech. She too is kinda short. She is about as tall as us, has short, curly gray hair, wears glasses with a round black frame, and has a suntan. She also has VERY RED lipstick on, and some of it is on her teeth, but I will keep that to myself! I don't want to embarrass Miss Meatball. That would not be nice. She reminded me of my 3rd grade teacher, Mrs. Franklin, since she wears glasses, and they were down to her nose like Mrs. Franklin's used to be!

"Ok campers, if you do not have any questions, please remain at your tables and your counselor will make their way over to meet you. Also, all meals will be served in the circus tent. Breakfast is from 8 a.m. to 9 a.m., lunch is from 12 p.m. to 1 p.m. and dinner is 5 p.m. to 6 p.m. Every day will be full of planned activities and in the evenings, after dinner, we will have game nights, movie nights, and all the fun that you can expect to have during summer camp. All schedules will be placed inside your cabins daily. Housekeeping will be done daily to refresh towels and straighten up cabins. Please check the schedule each morning to know which activity your cabin has been assigned to for the day. Please be respectful of all campers. If you have any issues with anything or anyone, please report it immediately to your cabin camp counselor. Campers, we are going to have the best time, but always remember, safety is first and foremost. Please abide by all rules and regulations of the camp. Be a good friend, and camp roommate. Clean up after yourselves and have fun!"

Oh my gosh, when are they going to stop going over the rules! UGH we get it! Behave!! Listen, and don't do anything dumb! Ha-ha! I am very serious about following the rules, but they left all camp information in our cabins, which we will review so let's get this party started!

Wait . . . is that . . . wait . . . what's on the menu for dinner? CHEESE PIZZA!!??!! YES and french fries?! Yipppeeeee!! Are you kidding me! It's like they read my diary and know everything about me!!! YES!!! Cheese pizza for alllllllll!! Ok, so far camp is awesome! You throw some cheese pizza at me and I'm ready for anything. I had 3 pieces of pizza and a bowl of French fries with RANCH! YUP! Good Old Ranch dressing!! Who's with me on that one? I need to write a song about Ranch Dressing!

"Ranch Dressing is the best. It sure is the best in the West." Well, I live in the Southeast, so I need to work on that song! Ha- ha!

After we had dinner, it was time for our parents to leave camp. All I kept thinking was, *"don't cry, Maggie, don't cry, Maggie."* I held on to my mom like I never did before. I wasn't ready for her to leave, but she needed to go. All campers parents were instructed to leave after dinner. I gave my mom a HUGE kiss on the cheek, one more extra tight hug and we all headed back to our cabins. We were ok. Little sad, but once Haley burped we all started laughing and that was it   I guess it was time to have some fun at camp as we would see our parents in 5 days, so let's make the best of circus camp while we are here!

We took showers, brushed our teeth, and we all jumped into our beds. My roommates at camp seem nice. Note to self, don't fart when sleeping or Haley will not be happy, but other than that, hoping that we have a fun 5 days! Miss Meatball seemed really nice, too. I'm still thinking that's a made-up name, but I dunno. She unpacked all of her stuff, and she came in to our room to say "goodnight." We filled her in on where we were from and stuff like that. I'm tired, and we have a busy day tomorrow. I'm off to bed. Good night from circus camp!

Love, Maggie

Rae Marsh

July 16th

Holy smokes, what is that noise? Is that a bugle horn thingy? It's so loud! I thought this was circus camp, not military camp! It's 7 A.M.! The sun isn't even really up yet, and there's a horn blarin' in our ears? Yikers! I thought roosters were supposed to wake people up super early, not horns! Ha-ha! ! What 9-year-old wants to get up at 7 A.M.?!! Why did my parents do this to me? I'm so sleepy.

    We all get up, still half asleep, and pulling ourselves out of our bunk beds! We all brush our teeth and we allllll have braces!! Wash our faces, get dressed and are ready to start the day!

    We see our schedule on the kitchen table. It says, "Today's cabin activity: Trapeze!"

    GULP! Trapeze!!!??? I'm flying through the air on day one!? What the heck! I thought I would have something easier to start with like juggling or being a mime but going right into the Trapeze??!! Oh my gosh! I hope my mom packed kneed pads and that helmet! Ha-ha!

    We headed over to the kitchen tent and had our breakfast. They had a buffet set up so campers could select from orange juice, milk, or water, and to eat they had a variety of cereals, waffles, scrambled eggs and bacon. I ate all choices! Ha-ha AND I had chocolate milk. It was so yummy, but after I ate I was thinking . . . maybe I shouldn't have eaten so much since I'm going to be swinging around in the air . . . Uh oh . . . this could have a bad outcome. EEKS!! Stomach don't fail me now! Heading over to the circus tent . . . toot, toot, toot, tooooooooot. Oh my goodness, I shouldn't have had so many eggs! STINKKKKKY!!! Thank goodness they were silent toots!

We get into the big circus tent and inside it smells like POOP! Like actual POOP! We were all like, "What in the world? That smell!"

Miss Meatball said, "Girls, we have elephants at circus camp. We clean up their droppings daily, BUT the stink kinda stays behind even after their droppings are is gone! Sorry!!" Ha-ha!

"Ok, Miss Meatball we will hold our noses." I should've known it would stink *IN* the circus tent because the pathways smell like POO!

We have 4 instructors for the trapeze. Mr. Drew, Miss Stacy, Miss Brooke and Miss Amy. They are all trapeze specialists. They suit us up in our safety gear, which is a safety belt around our waists, tell us the instructions for how to trapeze correctly, and then we are ready to go . . .

What? They think we are ready to go? The only thing I am ready to do is have diaherrea! Ha-ha! I'm so nervous! Ok, it's now or never! let's do this!!!! I was singing the "trapeze song" in my head . . .

"Weeeeee fly through the air, with the greatest of ease, we are daring young campers ONNNNNN the flying trapeze   " That *really is* a song, but I don't know the words! We have to climb up a ladder that literally looks like it's going to go through the top of the tent, it's so high!

My roommates and I tried to decide who would go first. NO ONE wanted to go first! Ok   Rock, Paper, Scissors it is!! Me and Haley first   OH Brother, I lost that round, scissors cut paper! Why do I always pick paper when everyone always choses scissors!! UGH MAGGIE!! Well, after all of the rounds completed, guess who lost? The one, the only   ME!! Oh no!!!

I can do this, right? Sure I can! YES I can!! I will just go verrrrryyyy slowly up the ladder   I counted each and every step up on the ladder . . . 5, 10, 20   Oh my goodness, when will I reach the top? 25, 30, and finally after reaching 50 steps, I make it to the top of the ladder.

When I get there, there is a teeny platform to stand on. Why is this thing so small? My feet won't fit on this thing. It's the size of a piece of paper that I write my "to do" list on!!! Next to the platform there is another platform with a safety person. I was already latched into a safety hook, but they latched me in again to another hook. Miss Stacy was the one who latched me in.

I hear my roommates below screaming "Go Maggie!! You got this Maggie!!"

"Ok Maggie, on the count of 3, I want you to lean forward and push off. Once you push off, you will be able to swing back and forth"

"I'm scared, Miss Stacy."

"Nothing to be afraid of, honey. You are safely buckled in, and there is a safety net below. You will be fine. It will be a lot of fun. Give it a try, Maggie"

"Ok, on the count of three, lets say it together . . . one . . . two . . . threeeeee . . ."

"Ahhhhhhhhhhh . . . ahhhhhh . . . stop swinging . . . I'm too high . . . ahhhhhhh . . . stop this swinging!"

Then, I stopped. I swung to the other side. Miss Amy grabbed my safety harness and pulled me onto the platform.

That. Was. Amazing!!!! My roomies went after me, and they loved it too! Oh my gosh, it was so much fun!!!! Scary, but fun! Yahoo! Lets do that again!

It was such a fun day at camp. When I lost at Rock, Paper, Scissors, I was so scared because I didn't want to go first on the trapeze. but my parents always tell me when you have the ability to try something once, try it, and if you don't like, you do not need to do it again. I told Haley, Emily and Emma how scared I was, and they said they would be there to cheer me on, and that we would all get through it together, and once we did it one time, we would probably want to do it again, but if not, at least we tried something new.

I just met these 3 girls, and it was like we knew each other for a lot longer. It's like we had each other's backs, just like my friends at home. The girls didn't realize how much better they made me feel. I was so scared to be away from my family for the first time, and now to be trying something new without my family. It's scary, but It felt like a home away from home in that moment. Super cool. Turns out that I like meeting new friends, and I'm really enjoying this circus camp experience!

I'm so tired. We had cheeseburgers for dinner tonight with smiley french fries and coconut cream pie. It was so yummy. Good night! Busy day at camp tomorrow! It's elephant day . . . whatever that means! Ha-ha!

Love, Maggie

"Say what, Mr. Elephant Man?!! Ride? What did you say? I am *NOT* riding an elephant!"

Love, Maggie

"Da Da Da DAAAAAAAA!" 7 A.M. already!!!?? Is that horn or bugle thing getting louder? It can't be 7 A.M.! I feel like I went to sleep 10 minutes ago! BUT today is elephant day for our cabin!! Today we are partnering up with two other cabins so there will be 12 of us for elephant day.

We get to the kitchen tent, and we all had cereal this morning, nothing fancy as we were so excited to find out what "elephant day" is . . . probably just sitting and watching elephants do tricks or maybe we would be able to feed them peanuts . . . hopefully something fun!

We ate our cereal, and I had some orange juice, and at 8 a.m. sharp, Miss Meatball takes us over to the BIG circus tent. There are several tents at camp . . . trapeze was tent #1. This is the BIG circus tent and the largest of all tents! It's pink with blue, orange, yellow, green and other colored stripes! The top has a carousel on it! Not a real one, but still, it looks like an actual carousel!

We walk into the tent and the floor is all dirt, so it's kinda dusty in the tent. I like to call it "dirt dusty." They have some bleachers set up and all of the campers sat down. We waited for about 5 minutes and all of a sudden, 3 GIANT elephants come out of an area in the back, and their trunks go up and they make the PUUUUUUUU UUUUUUUUU sound! Super loud. It was so cool!! All three elephants and the trainers were standing next to them. I didn't see any peanuts.

"Good morning, Campers! I am Mr. Smiley, the head trainer of the Elephants. To my right is Miss Samantha, and to my left is Mr. Jones! We are all excited to welcome you to elephant day here at circus camp! This here is Mumbo, one of the largest elephants at circus camp, and he's very sweet! Miss. Samantha is the trainer for Jumbo, and he likes to eat tons of grass and plants. The youngest elephant is named . . . nope, it's not what you think it is . . . our youngest is Zumbo and you are going to be able to ride these elephants today!"

Say what, Mr. Elephant Man?!! Ride? what did you say? I am *NOT* riding an elephant!

Emily was like "YES!!! This is awesome!!" We thought she was cuckoo!!

First, the trapeze and then elephant riding? Next year's camp better be soccer camp or swim camp or maybe just relax camp . . . circus camp is too stressful!! Ha-ha!

All of the instructors were wearing tan shorts, tan shirts and tan hats that look like safari hats that people wear in jungle type of movies, and they all have big brown boots on. Actually, come to think of it, they look like the guys that deliver my mom's work package to the house every day.

Mr. Smiley said the elephants are like 10 feet in height and weigh 10,000 POUNDS!!! 10,000 POUNDS!!!! What!!?? That's a lot of pounds, people!

Miss Samantha explained about our groups . . . "Camper Group A and B, you will go to the left side of the tent to ride on Jumbo. Camper Group D, you will go to the right to ride on Zumbo."

We head to the right of the tent. The counselors give us helmets, knee pads, elbow pads, and gloves! Oye yoi yoi! Another ladder. There is a ladder that we need to climb just like the trapeze to the platform and then get onto the elephant.

"Excuse me Mr. Counselor? Do you have any treats like peanuts that we can give Zumbo if he does a good job?"

"They eat plants, honey. We do not have any peanuts as some campers have peanut allergies. We only feed the elephants plants as that is their main source of food."

Hmmmm that's good to know! I get to the top of the ladder. Zumbo was just hanging out waiting for me to jump on his back, I guess, and the counselor helped me onto Zumbo. Oh my gosh, it was so scary and fun all at the same time! I was shaking a little bit as I was so nervous, and my hands were really sweaty, but that feeling didn't last long. It was just incredible!! The campers were once again saying, "Go Maggie!! Yay Maggie!!" It was awesome!! Another accomplishment! His trunk was just flying around. I think he was trying to kiss me! He had super long eye lashes, they looked like curtains from where I was sitting. He was so wrinkly, but super cute and very calm. I felt like I was riding on my doggie, GG! Zumbo was this huge gentle elephant that was so sweet, like he wanted a hug. I loved riding Zumbo!

I am so proud of myself! I never thought I would ride an elephant!

I was extra super scared because I was the one who rode Zumbo first out of my friends! I cannot seem to get a "W" on rock, paper, scissors, but, speaking of rocks . . . circus camp rocks so far!!

I'm once again super duper tired! I had lasagna for dinner, with salad, and a couple of pieces of cheesy garlic bread. It was really good! For lunch they just give us a choice of different sandwiches, and I picked a turkey sandwich, with a few slices of pineapple, a snack pack bag of salt-n-vinegar potato chips and one delicious and chewy chocolate chip cookie! Hopefully pizza night will pop up again! Ha-ha!

Tomorrow is "learn to be a clown day." I'm sure Morgan would love this place, just kiddin'! Ha-ha! Good night my friends, and my new cutie and stinky friend Zumbo.

Love, Maggie

July 18th

After a good night's sleep, we once again wake up to a bugle, and still no rooster . . . where *is* this rooster?? Wasn't it in the circus camp flyer or something? Oh well, I don't know, but onto day 3 . . .

We entered the "world of clowns today!" Honestly, a bit spooky for me! There were 5 clowns and they were all dressed in large clown costumes. All really baggy clothes, down to their feet all the way up to their necks! It's soooo hot out, and we have to wear a turtle neck outfit? Holy cow that's gonna be hot. The costumes were all different colors and we were allowed to pick one . . . They didn't have a pink costume, so I chose yellow to match my hair color! They had several different colors, and they all had large round buttons going down the front, and some of them had white polka dots on them. They were funny looking, but cute at the same time. The clown instructors were all wearing large red clown shoes, which were like size 25! They looked like red canoes!!! Their makeup was white around their faces, and they had red diamonds painted around both eyes. They were huge red diamonds and then a large red smile, but creepy, like they

aren't really smiling . . . like a smirk. I dunno, but they had HUGE, poofy, curly wigs. The wigs were pink, yellow, blue and green and were super poofy. Three of the clowns were juggling orange tennis balls and the other two clowns were standing on chairs and balancing on one foot while playing the symbals! What the heck? Ha-ha! I can barely stand on one foot on the ground without falling over! How are they balancing with one foot on a chair? Geez, I hope we don't have to do that. My 9-year-old body can't hold up to much more of this circus stuff. It's hard work!

One of our clown instructors, Mr. Toby, said that clowns don't usually speak in the circus act, but today, he's going to chat with us about how they apply the makeup and get ready for each show. The only thing I could think of was how in the world do they stay quiet for so long? I can't keep quiet for 15 seconds! Ha-ha! Mr. Toby and the rest of the clown crew took the 4 of us into the makeup room and showed us how to apply the makeup and get our poofy wigs in place on our heads, and how to put our costumes on without tripping and falling over! They were so baggy and HUGE!!! We looked *SO* funny! The one clown showed us how to juggle and all we did was throw tennis balls up in the air and couldn't figure it out, so the juggling part was an EPIC FAIL! Ha-ha! We couldn't walk in the clown shoes, and just kept tripping and laughing. The costumes were so big on us! It was so much fun! We really enjoyed being a clown for a few hours. BUT, how in the world do we get out of these costumes and get all of this make up off??!! YIKERS!!

Clown day was fun! After we finished clowning around . . . I *had* to say that! Ha-ha, we went back to our cabin to shower.

Circus camp is full of so many different experiences. Last week I never would've thought that I would be riding on an elephant, and swinging on a trapeze or dressing like an actual clown!! I love this place, but my goodness it is tiring! We are all so tired at the end of each day from having so much fun!

For dinner tonight, we had fish and chips in the kitchen tent with a ton of Ranch!! Ha-ha! I cannot get enough Ranch dressing. I guess most people use tartar sauce, but I think tater sauce is gross, so Ranch dressing is the main food group of my life and should be used on everything that people eat! Ha-ha!

After our yummy dinner, we had movie night. It was a new movie about the circus and how a girl becomes a trapeze professional! Never heard of it, but why didn't I audition for this movie? I am probably a trapeze expert by now! I mean, I did fly around for 2 hours the other day! Ok, I will leave that to the pros!

This has been such a great week! I'm really having a good time with my roommates and doing all of these fun things together. BUT . . . I am really starting to miss my family and my lil' GG. I've been away for 3 days now, and it feels like a lot longer. I miss cuddling on the couch with my mom and arguing with Morgan! Ha-ha! I don't really miss arguing with Morgan, but I do miss seeing her! I miss GG jumping all over me in the morning and giving me slobbery kisses during the day. I also miss playing soccer with my dad in the backyard. My mom said that I could call her if I wanted to come home, but ya know what? I'm going to stick this out. Only a few more days of camp. I told my roommates that I was homesick, and they were too! We were all missing our homes and our families. After sharing our thoughts, we all felt so much better! We were going to support each other more, give each other hugs, and be our own circus family for a few more days. I realized tonight that it really helped me to share my thoughts and it's good to share, because you never know if one of your friends is feeling the same way. Plus, if they are good friends, they will support you and help you through it. You have to trust in people to help you through things. We told Miss Meatball that we were missing home, and she gave us all big hugs, and tucked us into bed like we were little kids. It was so nice. I needed that to get me through the rest of circus camp.

My roommates asked me what I write in my journal at night, and I just told them I write about thoughts, feelings, and experiences of the day so that I don't forget them. They thought my journal was really cool and they plan on getting one when they get home. I am so glad I have a diary. Some people call it a journal.

I'm so tired. Good night. Maybe the rooster will be around tomorrow morning.

Love, Maggie

"Once again, it came down to the most trusted decision making game for kids of all time . . . playing Rock, Paper, Scissors, to see who goes first."

Love, Maggie

"Da, Da, Da, DAAAAAAAA!!!"

Bugle? Really? Again? OMG! Ha-ha! That bugle is soooo annoying but it's starting to grow on me! Ha-ha! I still don't know who is blowing the bugle or horn. It comes through a speaker in our cabin.

It's now day 4 of camp . . . the final days of circus camp are upon us and today, it's allll about water skiing! I have no idea why water skiing is part of circus camp, but it is, and I cannot wait! They have a wave pool here to teach us surfing too!!! YIPPPEEEE!!!YAHOOO!!! I totally forgot to write it down in my diary! The camp counselors told us yesterday during movie night. They made an announcement that the last two days of circus camp would be allllll about water skiing in the lake and surfing in the wave pool!! NICE!! This is my kinda camp! Love me some water sports, and fun in the sun! No more stinky circus tents, but I do kinda miss the elephants. They were so cute, and their trunks sounded like trumpets, and we all know that Maggie

Montgomery (aka Maggie Fun-Fun), loves her trumpet!!!

My roomies and I had breakfast together in the kitchen tent. We all had pancakes that were shaped like elephants today! They were so cute! We added a bunch of syrup and whipped cream! Deeeelicious!!! Then we washed our hands and headed over to the lake with Miss Meatball!

The lake is named "Take a Dippidy Lake!" Ha-ha! The instructors provided us sunscreen, and we all looked like ghosts, we put so much on and we couldn't get it to rub in our faces!

Even though we can all swim, we had to wear life jackets. We need to be safe in the lake!

There are 6 instructors for the lake activities and they're all lifeguards. They teach both water skiing and will be with us for surf lessons tomorrow! Oh my gosh and I can't wait for surfing!!!

The one guy kept saying, "This is totally rad campers; you are in for soooo much fun on the water the next two days!"

He was from California and his name was Cody!!! Remember Cody from my winter ski trip in 3rd grade? Well now I have a summer water ski instructor named Cody too! He was cool. He told us what we needed to do to stand up on water skis and to actually be able to ski around the lake without falling. We were going one at a time and no tricks were allowed! Tricks? I just want to stand on these skis without wiping out!!

Who the heck is going to do a trick? Like a double back flip or something? Ha-ha! This Cody guy is making me laugh. We are 9-year-olds, not professional water skiers!

Once again, it came down to the most trusted decision making game for kids of all time . . . playing Rock, Paper, Scissors, to see who goes first   It is the only game on Earth that is fair in a kids mind! Ha-ha and guess who WON?!...YUP!! Me!!! This time, I selected paper, and paper actually came out for the WIN!! Yay!

Since I won the game, I decided to go last. Haley is first, followed by Emma, then Emily, and then me. Haley took off and was up for about 2 seconds. Emma decided not to do it!! What? She was scared that she would fall and hurt herself, and the instructors wanted her to feel comfortable, so they didn't force her into doing it! Emily didn't get off of the land!! Ha-ha! She literally stood there, her helmet on, her skis pointing out and she was holding onto the water ski handle and when the boat driver said,

"You ready?"

Emily said, "No, thank you! I don't want to go." and dropped the handle and walked away!! Ha-ha!

My turn!! Yay! I was all ready to go! Give me that handle, Cody, let's get this show on the road . . . Well let's get this show on the WATER!!

"Ok Maggie are you ready!"

"YES!!! Let's go!! I'm ready"

"OK! HOLD ON TIGHT"

"OK . . . ahhhhhhhhhhhhhhhhhhhhhhhh . . ." Oh my gosh! Slow down boat driver man!!

"Ahhhhhhhhhhhhhhhh," uh oh, here comes the waves from the boat and I am tooting up a storm!!! "Ahhhhhhhhhhh!" Skis, don't fail me now! Jumped over one wave, jumped over another, and then . . . WIPE OUT!!!! UGH!!

Water up my nose, and I couldn't see a thing!! The boat driver circled around to pick me up in the water.

"You ok, Maggie?"

"YES! That was so much fun!!!!"

Mr. Boat driver (we literally did not know his name), got me back into the boat and took me back to shore.

The campers were all yelling "Yay Maggie! Awesome job!!"

It felt so good!! Once Emily saw me go, she asked Cody if she could go too! She was scared, and now seeing that I had fun and was safe, she decided to go too!

I was proud of my new friend Emily, and once she got suited up, she was up on her skis for about 5 seconds, and she had a blast!! Sometimes you just have to watch another friend go first to make you feel comfortable trying something new and that's OK! She loved it and was so happy that she didn't miss out on the water skiing fun!

Emma still was a hard NO! She wanted nothing to do with it! Ha-ha, my camper friends are fun and silly!

OMG, I can't wait for surfing tomorrow!! They seemed to have saved the best for the last day!! Can't wait!!

I'm so tired from all of these activities. After skiing, we headed to the kitchen tent for dinner. Dinner was good tonight too! We had a taco bar! Alllll the taco night fixings: meat, cheese, sour cream, lettuce, tomatoes, you name it, they had it. I limited my amount of beans for Haley's sake! Ha-ha! I didn't want to be tooting all night in the bunk bed above her!! We also played a few board games like Chutes and Ladders and Candy Land. No matter how old you get, those are board games are always favorites! Thank goodness they didn't have Scrabble. My parents would've loved it though!

Good night! Rooster, you ever gonna show up at this camp? Ha-ha!

Love, Maggie

"What the heck was that? If that was surfing, I do not want to get back in line!! That was so funny!! Wow! I am a terrible surfer!!"

Love, Maggie

"Da Da DA DAAAAAAAAA!!!!!"

7 A.M., let's go!!!!! Surf time peeps!!! I have been sleeping so well at circus camp, but I think it's because I am so tired at night! Last night's sleep wasn't as good though, as I was tossing and turning in excitement! Thinking about surfing!! Today is going to be the best day yet . . . OH YEA!!! LET'S GOOOOOOOO!! I was picturing myself on a pink board, with my pigtails blowin' in the wind, riding the waves towards the shore with my friends cheering me on. It's probably going to be *EXACTLY* like that! I know it will be! Even though I have never been surfing before, I am athletic. How hard can surfing be, right? My cabin roommates were super excited too! We got up, threw on our bathing suits, brushed our teeth and braces, and headed to the kitchen tent for the start of the day! Miss Meatball was with us too, of course. She said that she had a really good night's sleep as she was exhausted from the last few days of camp!

That sounds like something my mom would say . . . "I'm so tired from watching all of the stuff you guys did but didn't do anything!" Ha-ha!

Today we had a selection of cereals, fruits and French toast! I love me some French toast ever since my dad made it, so I loaded that up with syrup and a big blast of whipped cream. I did throw a couple strawberries on top to make it "healthy," and I also had some cinnamon cereal; that's my favorite!! OHHHHH I love me some cinnamon cereal!

After our bellies are full, we are now on our way to go surfin'!!! Yay!! OH MY GOSH I *CANNOT* WAIT!!! We had to take a small tram over to the wave pool as it was about ½ mile away from the other circus activity tents. The long tram was orange with black stripes on it, like a tiger. If they had tigers here, I would've hidden in my cabin underneath the couch! Ha-ha! Lions and tigers are sccccaaaarrrryyyyyy!

Today we were partnered up with the campers of Cabin C, and we headed over to the wave pool together! YES!!! Can't wait for this!! After the tiger tram dropped us off, we had just a few yards to go, and we were running, skipping and high fiving! YES, surfing!! Here we come!!

We arrived at the pool, and it's a HUGE pool! It looks like the size of a football field, but it wasn't *that* big, but it was big! The smell of sunscreen and chlorine surrounded the area. There was a large area in front of the wave pool that they made into a beach. It was full of sand, and there were about 50 sun chairs scattered around the beach. All of the sun chairs were white, and there were sun umbrellas attached to each chair for shade. Every single umbrella was a different color. I didn't even know there were 50 colors that could be made into umbrellas! It was so pretty! Pink umbrellas, light blue, dark blue, light green, yellow, you name it, they had it, and some had polka dots on them! I love polka dots! There were two white towels on each chair with a small side table next to the chair to place a drink and a snack.

While we were checkin' out the beach, we heard a *really* loud horn sound "HOOOONNNKKKKKKK" which startled all of us   Then, all of a sudden, the water in the wave pool starts to slush up and down and waves become bigger and bigger! Two of the instructors "caught a wave" and rode it on to the shore!! It was so awesome! Miss Meatball told us that the horn sounds every 7 minutes to signal to the staff and campers that a new wave will begin in the wave pool. The staff can make the entire pool have waves, OR they can make one BIG wave! SO COOL!! Since it is surfing today, they are setting the wave pool up for large waves only so that we can surf! They said most of the waves will be about 6-8 feet tall. Since we are under 5 feet tall that sounds like a good start!

Cody was an instructor for surfing since he is in charge of water activities. There were 3 other lifeguards that were going to watch us for safety. Miss Amy, from the big tent, will be assisting Cody with the surf lessons and she began the surf meeting . . .

"We need each of you to grab a sun chair please. We will sit for a few minutes to review the rules of the surfing lesson. On each chair is a pink life jacket. Please make sure to put your life jacket on now. Cody and I will be checking life jackets to make sure they are on correctly. Next to your chairs, you will find sunscreen. Please make sure to put on *a LOT* of sunscreen on all over your face and body so you do not get a sunburn! There is also a bucket full of ice with water bottles. We need to make sure you stay hydrated campers, as it's going to be a hot day today and very sunny. We will have our lunch on our chairs while covered under our umbrellas. The bathrooms are over to the right of the wave pool."

Oh my gosh!! C'mon!!! Us kids want to surf!! Ok Ok, we get it, if we need to pee, it's over there, we need to drink water, we have sunscreen . . . let's do this!

Once they get us all situated with the rules of surfing, sunscreen, lunch orders, drink orders, etc., we are ready to rock-n-roll! FINALLY!! It only took 15 minutes or so for them to tell us the rules, but it honestly seemed like 3 ½ days! UGH! Parents, teachers, and now counselors going on and on . . . Ha-ha! Safety first, though, we have got to be safe.

"Ok Campers, time get started! Line up according to cabins, and we will check your life jackets. After securing the life jackets, you can proceed to the top of the wave pool."

Here we go, again!!! Ha-ha . . . Rock, Paper, Scissors and guess who went first?!!! ME!!! I did!!!

This time, I went with the rock which seems to win most of the time, in my experience playing the game, but that's completely my opinion. I do not think there has been a study conducted on the outcomes of the rock winning in rock, paper, and scissors! Ha-ha!

The counselors had us lay our surf boards on the sand, and they gave us a quick rundown on how to surf. This is what I heard . . . "Do this, do that, do this, then that." OK, got it!! Let's surf . . . like now! Ha-ha!

I head to the top of the wave pool, and my pink surfboard is . . . wait, yellow is not pink, but whatever, it has cute pink flowers on it. Miss Stacy only had two surf boards available. Cody was at the top as well.

"Ok, honey. When the horn goes off, you will have 30 seconds to catch a wave. If you cannot stand on the surfboard, you can lay on it and the wave will take you onto the beach. Do you understand, Maggie?"

"YES! I sure do! Let's do this! Honk that wave horn please!"

"Ok Maggie, here we go!"

All I could think of was, "I can do this, I can do this."

The horn sounds, "HOOOOOONNNNKKKKK!" The wave pool starts, I get into the water with my yellow board, and "AHHHHHHHH" what is happening!!! Why am I spinning around on the board? I'm supposed to be going straight towards the beach while "surfing a wave . . ."

"Ahhhhhhhhhhhhh!! Ahhhhhhh!!! Ugggggg!!" and splat onto the beach!!

What the heck was that? If that was surfing, I do not want to get back in line!! That was so funny!! Wow! I am a terrible surfer!! My friends were laughing so hard when I splatted onto the sand. My board went one way and I face planted. I got up and there was sand all over my face, in my pigtails and lodged into the dimple in my chin! Sand was *everywhere* and probably stuck in my braces too! Yikers!!!

Emma loved surfing! She got on the board, fell off, and kept doing the same thing over and over again. Emily wanted to lay out in the sun, so she didn't even try, and Haley LOVED it too! She couldn't catch a wave, but she had fun in the water! With her being from Alaska, she doesn't get much summertime fun, so she was willing to try it, and she had so much fun!! Such an awesome day of surfing and hanging out in the wave pool! We had Shirley Temples, water, iced tea, and cheese quesadillas for lunch. They didn't have Ranch dressing, but I did have sour cream on it! We also had ice cream sandwiches that literally melted in 8 seconds because it was so hot out, but they were yummy!

After surf lessons, we got back on the tiger tram and headed to our cabins to shower and get ready for our last dinner at camp. Tonight is going to be extra fun because we are having a campfire!! We are going to roast marshmallows, make s'mores, and tell scary stories! It's going to be fun!

We kinda had a scary situation on the way back to our cabin though. After we got off of the tram and started walking down the path to our cabin, we had to stop. Emily had a terrible headache and needed to sit down. We were so worried about her! Her sister Emma told us that sometimes Emily gets headaches, and they are so awful, that she has to take medicine for them. Her headaches are called migraines. I never heard of that. Miss Meatball was with us. She called the camp medical staff, and they came out to us in a golf cart. They gave Emily some water and laid her down on the bench under a tree for a few minutes with a cold compress on her head. Emily told the medical people that she had her headache medicine in the cabin. The best thing for her to do was to lay down in a dark room because light was bothering her too. We felt so bad for Emily!

"Emily, is there anything we can do to help?"

"It's ok Maggie, my head starts to hurt, and I need to take my medicine and rest. No loud noises or anything either. I will be OK. I'm sorry I will miss the campfire."

We were sorry too. It was such a bummer, but we knew that Emily needed to rest, so a campfire wasn't going to do her any good either. Sometimes we have to miss out on fun activities, but we need to remember that our friends miss us when we aren't at fun events with them. If we have to miss fun stuff, there will be other fun things that we will be able to participate in, and

it's OK to miss things sometimes. Don't be sad, just look forward to being at the next fun activity with friends!

    We got back to the cabins, and we had to pack before we did anything else, as tomorrow we were all going home! I sure am going to miss everyone that I met at camp, especially my cabin buddies, but I CANNOT WAIT to see my family! I miss lil' GG jumping on me every morning and I am super excited to tell my family allllll about camp and how much fun it was!!

After packing, *which seemed to take FOREVER,* we all took quick showers and Miss Meatball walked with us over to the campfire site. It was SO COOL! It was HUGE!!! Cody and some of the other lifeguards and camp instructors set up a few logs around the fire pit. They had music playing from a boom box that looked like something my parents would listen to music on 100 years ago! Ha-ha! We all took a seat around the campfire. Everyone had their choice of hot cocoa or milk to drink. The counselors passed out metal sticks to each of us to roast our marshmallows and each of us had 6 marshmallows, 2 large graham cracker squares and one bar of milk chocolate!! An entire bar of chocolate! Yuuummmmmyyyyy!!! Smore's are going to be going down into my belly and safe to assume, a stomachache and then some nighttime toots will occur!! Oh well, a little bit of stinky gas never hurt anyone. The s'mores were deeeeeelicious! I had 4 of them and that was plenty with a glass of milk.

Cody turned off the music and we all shared what the best part of camp was. Emma said trapeze day. She enjoyed everyone flying around. Miss Meatball said that she enjoyed getting to know all of us and that she couldn't pick a day that was better than any other day. When it was my turn, I said that surfing was my favorite, and that I hope I could do it again sometime. Cody said he enjoyed every single thing about camp this year. All of the counselors said that we were a really good group of campers. They said that we were respectful and caring to each other and kind. That made me feel so good! I'm glad that the counselors had fun like we did!! After sharing, we turned the music back on and danced, we were singing loudly, and had *THE* best time!

I sure am going to miss everyone from Circus Camp, but I can't wait to see my family tomorrow!

It's getting late and my eyeballs are starting to close while I am writing in my journal! Nighty night surfer dudes!

Love, Maggie

"I got into the car, turned my head around and waved goodbye to the 'Skippidity Dippidty Doooooo' circus camp, and was just bursting with excitement!"

Love, **Maggie**

July 21st

Rise and Shine! Guess what? I heard the rooster!!! Turns out that the rooster actually does exist!!! We heard there was a rooster, BUT we never actually *heard* the rooster! Ha-ha!

"Cockadoodledooooooooooo . . . Cockadoodledooooooo . . ." Ok rooster, we are up, calm down! Ha-ha.

I wish GG were here to wake me up, but she can wake me up tomorrow!! Yipppeee!!! Now I understand when adults say things are "bittersweet." We will miss our friends from camp when we leave, but we are excited to get home, so one thing we will miss, but one thing we are excited about . . . is that what that phrase means? I dunno! I think so, but I'm not exactly sure. I need to ask my mom!

All of us are up after the rooster went crazy! Ha-ha! Emily is feeling so much better! She said that she no longer has a headache, and the extra sleep and resting helped out a lot! I guess when parents say to lay down and rest when we aren't feeling well, really can help us to feel better. I need to make sure that when I am not feeling well, I will just take it easy, and lay down on my couch or bed. I think we should all remember to do that. Our parents know what's best!

After I woke up, I stretched, I brushed my stinky teeth, washed my face and got dressed. I put on the cutest pink sundress today since I was going home! We are supposed to have a farewell breakfast at 8 a.m. in the circus tent, but we need to make sure all of our stuff is packed and ready to go. My mom always gives me a checklist for packing to go somewhere, and then I take the checklist with me to make sure I pack everything to take back home. It worked out great when we went on our ski trip last winter, as I almost forgot my sneakers at the hotel, but when I noticed that they were not checked off of my list, I found them under my bed in the bedroom! As I have told you all before, peeps, my mother LOVES a good list!! Ha-ha! Here we go . . .

   1) Pillow, check!
   2) Blanket, check!
   3) Dirty clothes, check!
   4) Toothbrush, check!
   5) Shoes, check!
   6) Deodorant, check check! Double check that deodorant! I don't want to smell like Zumbo! Ha-ha!

All packed and ready for our last camp breakfast . . . you could smell breakfast coming out of the tent and into the trail . . . smells like syrup and eggs. I smell onions too, which is gross, but I can smell them!

The 4 of us and Miss Meatball get in line for the buffet, grab a plate, and what is it that I see?? YES!!!! It's Pancake Day!!! I don't know why I get so excited for pancakes, but they are just one of the best breakfast foods on planet Earth!! OMG, pancakes and they have chocolate sauce, whipped cream, strawberry sauce and sprinkles!! Holy smokes, my sugar levels are going to blow through the circus tent! Well, on the last day of camp, it's ok to eat all of it, but not every single day, that wouldn't be good for me, but every once in a while it's OK to have all the fixings on my pancakes!!! Pancakes, scrambled eggs with cheddar cheese, white toast with some butter and I added grape jelly, glass of chocolate milk! Best breakfast ever! This looks SO GOOD!!!

While we were stuffing our faces, Miss Meatball took the stage. That lady sure does love a microphone! Ha-ha! She wished all of the campers a great end of the summer and to please stay in touch and visit again next year!

We were done with breakfast and our cabin crew said our goodbyes to the rest of the campers. Some of us wrote our addresses down so that we can be pen pals and write to each other, and some of us shared phone numbers if we had a device to call each other on.

When we left the tent, I looked up, and YAY!!!! It's my mom and dad!!!!!!!! I ran to them!

"Hi MOM! Hi DAD! I missed you so much!"

"HI MAGGIE BEAR!! We missed you too, honey! We missed you so much! Morgan missed you and so did GG. WE can't wait for you to tell us about camp!"

It was a tighter hug then the one when they dropped me off! My parents were so excited to see me and I was over the moon excited to see them too! I can't wait to get home!

I walked with my parents to our cabin. Emily, Emma and Haley, and I all gave each other big hugs and we promised to keep in touch and would try to do another camp together next year.

Miss Meatball was crying. "You girls are the best. I will miss you so much!"

"We will miss you too, Miss Meatball!"

I got into the car, turned my head around and waved goodbye to the 'Skippidity Dippidty Doooooo' circus camp, and was just bursting with excitement! Not only was I extremely excited to see my mom and dad, but I also couldn't wait to tell them all of the details about my new circus camp friends, the activities we did, and the food we ate! There is SO much to tell them!!

"Mom, I don't know where to start."

"Maggie, start from day one and then go from there. We want to hear EVERY single detail about camp!!"

Good thing is, you all know how much I LOVE to talk, so when someone says they want to hear "every single detail," that's my JAM! Ha-ha!

It was such a fun car ride home. I spilled alllll of the summer camp beans, and about 70 minutes later, we pulled into the garage, and I said,

"By the way, how was your week, mom and dad? Ha-ha! I talked the ENTIRE TIME from camp to our house!!! The *ENTIRE* time!! Ha!"

My mom said, "Honey, we had a good week too. Morgan hung out with Annie and played some soccer and went swimming. Your dad and I worked, but we did have one thing really exciting happen!"

"What mom? What was exciting?"

"I will tell you when we get into the house"

"OK!"

We open the door to the house and GG attacks me!!! GG GG!! NO!!!! Hahahahahah GG!!!! Hahahaha! GGGGGGG! OMG G! I love you too G! I missed you so much too G!! G get off of me!! ha-ha!!

"Hi Maggie! How was camp?"

"Hi Morgan! It was so much fun!! OH MY GOSH!! What are you holding??!! Where did you get that puppy!!!??? Why are you holding a puppy!? What is going on?!!!"

"Well, Maggie, that was the one exciting thing that happened while you were gone! Since you and your sissy kept asking for another puppy and for GG to have a friend, we decided to adopt another dog . . . her name is River."

I was sobbing. I was so excited! I couldn't believe it!!

"She's alllll ours?"
"Yes! She is our new family member and she's a cutie."

River looks EXACTLY like GG!! She's like 8 pounds and has black short hair with a white and gray chest like a tuxedo! She literally looks exactly like GG, but in tiny puppy form!! Oh my gosh, my parents bought her a little bed, and she ate all of the stuffing out of it, so it looks like a flat gray rug now! Ha-ha! They bought her a bunch of squeaky toys, but she only likes to eat our shoes, and the best part about all this??? GG is ignoring her!! Oh brother!! I know just how River feels . . . I have a big sissy too, Rivy . . . Morgan ignores me too! Ha-ha!

I cannot believe we have a new puppy! I'm going to call her my lil' Rivy. It's so wonderful to have 2 dogs!! My parents said it's already a lot of work. I plan on helping out. I always want to help, but then I kinda don't! I need to get better at the helping thing as families should always help each other.

I am so tired from talking so much today!! Is that possible? Getting tired from talking too much?

This has been the GREATEST. SUMMER. EVER!!! I am so happy to be back home with my family, my GG and my new little puppy Rivy!

I can't believe that school starts in 2 short weeks!!! 4th grade, here I come!!!

Love, Maggie

Rae Marsh

"4th grade, here I come!!!"
Love, **Maggie**

Made in the USA
Coppell, TX
30 December 2025

67568760R00066